The XLISP Primer

BONNIE J. FLADUNG

PRENTICE-HALL, INC.
ENGLEWOOD CLIFFS, NEW JERSEY 07632

Library of Congress Cataloging-in-Publication Data

FLADUNG, BONNIE J.   (date)
    The XLISP Primer.

    Includes index.
    1.   XLISP (Computer program language)   I. Title.
QA76.73.X55F53 1987   005.13'3   87-2515
ISBN 0-13-972084-7

Editorial/production supervision and
    interior design: *Gloria Jordan*
Cover design: *Lundgren Graphics, Ltd.*
Manufacturing buyer: *S. Gordon Osbourne*

The publisher offers discounts on this book when ordered
in bulk quantities. For more information, write to:
    Special Sales/College Marketing
    Prentice-Hall, Inc.
    College Technical and Reference Division
    Englewood Cliffs, New Jersey 07632

Printed in the United States of America

10   9   8   7   6   5   4   3   2   1

ISBN   0-13-972084-7   025

Prentice-Hall International (UK) Limited, *London*
Prentice-Hall of Australia Pty. Limited, *Sydney*
Prentice-Hall Canada Inc., *Toronto*
Prentice-Hall Hispanoamericana, S.A., *Mexico*
Prentice-Hall of India Private Limited, *New Delhi*
Prentice-Hall of Japan, Inc., *Tokyo*
Prentice-Hall of Southeast Asia Pte. Ltd., *Singapore*
Editora Prentice-Hall do Brasil, Ltda., *Rio de Janeiro*

Dedicated to Danny, Margot, and Sam

Contents

Foreword

My first meeting with David Betz occurred during a computer show in Boston in October 1984. The Artificial Intelligence Special Interest Group of the Boston Computer Society was then only one year old. The biggest excitement of the computer show, for me, was the gift to the group by David Betz of a copy of his XLISP (version 1.2 at that time). This disk was used to start our Software Exchange.

For those members who were new to LISP, XLISP of even that early version was difficult to learn. I still remember my triumph when I finally unravelled the procedure for opening a file! Out of those frustrations came the need to have a tutorial dedicated to XLISP. A request to the members of the Artificial Intelligence Group was sent out in our monthly newsletter. It was with great delight that I received a preliminary response from Bonnie Fladung. After a few telephone calls, she made a firm commitment to perform the task.

The product of these efforts was an 80-page manuscript that Ms. Fladung gave the group permission to print and sell without royalty. That first manuscript was of such high quality that I have yet to receive any substantive criticisms, although nearly 300 copies have been sold by now. My perusal of the book before you indicates that the same high standard has been maintained in this more formal edition.

The release of this book and the availability of a companion and inexpensive version of LISP are particularly appropriate at this time. Interest in Artificial Intelligence and its tools is rapidly rising. The interest is not confined to higher institutions of learning and professionals. The telephone calls and letters that I receive daily record how many individuals with little or no computer expertise wish to learn about LISP. Most impressive of all was the call from a high school teacher who said his students had requested a course in LISP! To all such "beginners," Bonnie Fladung's book and David Betz's XLISP will provide a delightful welcome to the world of Artificial Intelligence.

Come and join us in the fun! And join us as well in an expression of deep gratitude to Bonnie Fladung and David Betz for easing the way.

Park S. Gerald, M.D.
Director, Artificial Intelligence Special Interest Group
Boston Computer Society

Preface

Software supporting artificial intelligence applications is becoming increasingly popular. Many of these applications are written in LISP. It is important for those people not familiar with the language to have a general idea of its features and functionality. This tutorial will expose you to the terminology and give you a working knowledge of the language. While this book can be used along with the XLISP interpreter diskette which David Betz has made available for noncommercial use, it can also stand alone as a simple tutorial guide and reference.

The tutorial is designed so that novice programmers can begin programming in LISP in a minimal amount of time. It will introduce LISP concepts that are difficult to understand if you have never programmed or have been programming in other languages. Many of the examples given are simple numeric problems that nonprogrammers can easily understand. Those programmers familiar with high-level languages such as BASIC or PASCAL will find this an excellent introduction to LISP and its unique programming style. As a teaching aid, XLISP provides a facility for saving an interactive session to a file that can be printed and saved for future reference.

This book also provides a complete reference guide for the XLISP interpreter, which is fairly compatible with Common LISP as documented by Guy Steele in *Common LISP*[1] and Winston and Horn in *LISP Second Edition*.[2] By actually using the XLISP inter-

[1] Guy L. Steele, Jr., *Common LISP* (Burlington, Mass.: Digital Press, 1984).

[2] Patrick Henry Winston and Berthold Klaus Paul Horn, *LISP, Second Edition*, (Reading, Mass.: Addison-Wesley Publishing Co., 1984).

preter along with this tutorial text, you will gain a deeper understanding of the language. Although David Betz has provided object-oriented programming capabilities with XLISP, it is beyond the scope of this manual to delve into this advanced subject matter.

The XLISP interpreter is available for noncommercial use and is, therefore, an inexpensive introduction to Common LISP. XLISP runs on many popular computers. Ordering information for obtaining the MS/PC DOS version of the diskette is provided in the back of this book.

ACKNOWLEDGMENTS

My sincere appreciation and thanks to those who encouraged and assisted me in this endeavor. To Park Gerald, who conceived the need for such a book and offered considerable support and encouragement throughout its development. To David Betz, who wrote the XLISP interpreter and generously made it available for noncommercial use. David's cooperation, suggestions, and critical comments were invaluable to the development of this tutorial. I would like to sincerely thank him for his permission to publish the information in the appendices, which summarize the XLISP language and its features. To my editor at Prentice-Hall, John Wait, who saw the need to publish a book describing the increasingly popular XLISP language. To Bert Horn, who carefully reviewed the manuscript and offered constructive criticisms. To all the members of the Boston Computer Society Artificial Intelligence Group who gave their suggestions. To Bill Hahn, for reasons that are obscure to me now.

A special thanks to my husband, Danny, for his patient reviews and critical comments on the book while it was in progress. And to Sam and Margot, who helped me organize my time productively and kept me company through the late nights.

Bonnie Fladung
New Hampshire

Introduction

PURPOSE OF THIS MANUAL

The purpose of this manual is to introduce the LISP programming language, with an emphasis on those functions compatible with Common LISP, which is rapidly becoming the standard used throughout education and industry.

This book will serve as a tutorial and reference manual for XLISP; the interpreter is available for noncommercial use. XLISP is migrating toward compatibility with Common LISP, although not all functions available in XLISP are currently implemented according to the rules of Common LISP as described by Guy Steele in *Common LISP*. The functions that differ are noted throughout this text.

WHY LISP?

What is the fascination with LISP, and how does it differ from other programming languages? It differs in several ways: It involves the processing of symbolic rather than numeric data; the data structures are highly flexible; and it encourages the use of recursion. Its highly interactive nature makes it a natural choice for developing software in an environment where rapid and innovative development is essential.

Symbolic data can be names, words, sentences, descriptions, and so forth, as opposed to working with numbers. LISP allows a computer to recognize and evaluate symbolic expressions of varying degrees of complexity.

Recursion is a programming technique. A *recursive function* will call itself in order to perform repetitive tasks. This technique is not available in some programming languages. A detailed description of recursion using ordinary examples is presented in this text.

Learning LISP   A basic set of skills must be acquired in order to use LISP effectively. These skills cannot be intuitively derived from a person's past experience with traditional computer languages.

Most novice programmers start out learning languages like BASIC, FORTRAN, or PASCAL. These languages are suitable for basic arithmetic functions, and programmers learn about numerical and character string processing. For more complicated data, however, the programmer using these languages is faced with an initial problem of how to represent the data using the data types available in the chosen language. Consider, for example, writing a program to multiply polynomials. The manipulation of symbolic data, such as sorting names and words, is based upon the algebraic nature of the specific language.

PROBLEM EXAMPLES

There are many problems that are difficult to program in languages other than LISP, such as the following:

1. Calculus problems involving symbolic differentiation or integration.
2. Programs that write and then execute programs based on input data. (It is difficult to imagine a *program* that writes executable programs, but this is possible in LISP.)
3. Problems involving "records" with an indefinite number of "fields." For example, an open-ended personnel database, where you might add information such as blood type and personality type on a weekly basis. These problems are difficult in a third-generation language since they are lacking in open-ended data structures. For example, in PASCAL you have to be very specific about the fields in a record. If you add a field, you have to recompile the program.
4. Problems involving symbolic data organized in recursive data structures, such as trees and queues.

The problem examples given above are all characterized by having data requirements that are difficult to define. The data in some of the examples will dynamically change in size and content as the program is executed. It would be difficult to tailor the data to fit into the arrays, numbers, characters, strings, and records available in most programming languages.

It is easier to attack these problems using LISP, since LISP allows us to group data together in lists. People make lists of things to do, such as shopping lists, and outline algorithms with lists of instructions. The list is a very natural data structure for humans, and it can be argued that the only reason it was not used at the dawn of computer languages was the lack of computing resources.

EFFICIENCY CONSIDERATIONS

A binary tree implemented with lists in LISP may be slower than a slick implementation done in PASCAL or assembly languages. There are two considerations, however, that enhance the decision to use LISP. The first is that hardware is improving all the time. The second is that very efficient programs written in other languages that utilize binary trees are difficult to write correctly. Also, their maintenance requires a larger manpower investment. New hardware can even make existing optimized code inefficient, if not detrimental to a system.

1

Getting Started with XLISP

THE DISKETTE

There are many versions of XLISP. This document specifically documents version 1.7, although it is designed in a generic manner so that it will be useful with previous versions as well as future upgrades. When you are ready to use the interpreter, consult the README.1ST file on your diskette for instructions from the author of XLISP on the contents and format of your specific diskette. Included on all versions of XLISP are files similar to the following (* indicates wild card):

README.1ST	XLISP author's instructions and index to diskette.
ARC.EXE	Executable file for extracting files from archive (see documentation in README.1ST for instructions).
XLISP.ARC	Archive containing files for XLISP interpreter (any of the files listed here may be archived depending upon the specific XLISP version).
XLISP??.EXE	XLISP executable file (the suffix ?? distinguishes among different executables if there is more than one on your diskette.
*.DOC	XLISP author's reference material (see Appendix A).

| *.LSP | XLISP source files containing sample user-defined functions provided by the author of XLISP. |
| *.C | C source files for XLISP interpreter. |

Throughout this document, the generic command ''xlisp'' is used to start the interpreter. For compatibility and ease of use, you may want to copy the XLISP executable you will be running into a file called XLISP.EXE.

A DISCUSSION ABOUT THE INTERPRETER

XLISP is an interpreted language like most BASICs. Any expression input at the terminal can be included in a program, and any expression in a program can be input directly from the terminal. The program evaluates the expressions it is passed, and returns a single value. If several expressions are entered on a line, the value of each expression is displayed on succeeding lines. The interpreter does not distinguish between upper- and lower-case characters.

An *expression* is anything that the evaluator is passed to evaluate and must be one of the valid data types defined in detail in the next chapter. You must hit the <return> key after typing in the expression in order for the interpreter to evaluate it. Writing and executing complex programs, as opposed to typing in simple expressions for evaluation, are discussed in a later chapter.

Parentheses are used often in LISP to denote function calls and list expressions. Many people have trouble reading and understanding LISP expressions due to the complexity of nesting many levels of parentheses within a function. Proper formatting to make expressions comprehensible is a necessity in LISP. Hopefully, as you become familiar and comfortable with the language, your parentheses phobia will disappear.

STARTING THE INTERPRETER

Start the interpreter by entering the correct executable program for your system (**?:xlisp,** where the prefix **?:** is the drive designator of the disk drive containing the XLISP program). This command loads the system files necessary to run the XLISP interpreter. The version number and date will appear.*

The ''>'' is the prompt character, which indicates that the interpreter is waiting for an expression to be typed. This is also referred to as *top-level* throughout this document. Expressions that you can type in and have evaluated will appear in **boldface** in the text.

EXITING THE INTERPRETER

You can exit the interpreter at any time by typing the expression (**exit**). Type <control-C> to return to top–level at any time. Type <control-B> to generate a breakpoint.

*XLISP version 1.7, Copyright © 1986, by David Betz

THE PROMPT LINE

After successfully evaluating an expression, the interpreter returns to the initial prompt line. However, certain conditions change the format of the prompt line. The prompt line indicates the number of errors you have generated as well as the number of incomplete expressions.

Some expressions in XLISP are entered between left and right parentheses. An incomplete expression is one in which the number of right parentheses does not match the number of left parentheses. The following expression is incomplete:

```
>  (+  2  3
1>
```

The integer preceding the prompt indicates that it is expecting 1 right parenthesis. At this point, you can enter the right parenthesis, and the interpreter will recognize that the expression has been completed. The interpreter will not evaluate any expressions until they are completed. Therefore, if you have entered

```
>  (+  2  3
1>
```

you must now enter the closing right parenthesis in order for the expression to be evaluated:

```
1>  )
5
>
```

ERROR MODE

Some versions of XLISP automatically put you in error mode when you generate an error. The error handler provides you with an error message and changes the format of the prompt line. When the error handler is invoked, you may be able to correct a mistake, for example, change the value of a variable and continue an evaluation. If you are a novice programmer, you will probably not want to deal with errors at this time. You can initialize the error mode by setting the system variable *breakenable* as follows:

```
> (setf *breakenable* NIL)      ;do not invoke error handler
NIL

> (setf *breakenable* T)        ;invoke error handler
T
```

In version 1.7, the default is NIL, and you will not enter the error handler. This tutorial assumes that *breakenable* is set to true. If you have set *breakenable* to false, or are working with a version of XLISP where the default is set to NIL, ignore the error messages that appear within the text that will not appear at your terminal.

ENTERING THE ERROR HANDLER*

If *breakenable* is T, then every time you generate an error, the interpreter invokes the error handler. In order to abort the error handler, the expression (clean-up) is used. This command only aborts the error handler one level. (On some systems, <control-Z> <return> will work similar to (clean-up).)

Successive (clean-up) or <control-Z> commands may be necessary to return you to the top-level if you have generated many errors. Throughout this book, (clean-up) is used to abort the error handler. The message [abort to previous level] will appear after you enter (clean-up).

If you want an immediate exit from the error handler back to the top-level, use <control-C> <return>. The message [back to the top level] will appear.

The interpreter also records the number of errors you have generated. An error has the following format where the word "error:" is followed by an explanatory message, and the subsequent line shows the number of errors you have generated thus far:

```
error: message
1:>
```

At this time, you need only be aware that the integer value preceding the : (colon symbol) indicates the number of errors you have generated. In order to return to the initial prompt, also referred to as top-level, enter (clean-up) (or <control-Z> if your system allows), followed by return for each error generated. Techniques to use the error-handling mechanism as a means of debugging your programs are discussed in a later chapter.

The following example demonstrates an error generated by passing the absolute value function more than the acceptable number of arguments:

```
> (abs 1 2)
error: too many arguments - (ABS 1 2)

1:> (clean-up)
[abort to previous level]
>
```

SUMMARY OF PROMPT LINE FORMATS

The prompt can show a combination of the number of errors and the number of missing right parentheses. The integer preceding the : denotes the number of errors and the integer following the : denotes the number of incomplete expressions.

*Skip this section if *breakenable* is NIL.

The prompt line has one of the following formats:

> \>   initial prompt (top-level)
> n>   *n* incomplete expressions
> x:>   *x* errors
> x:n>   *x* errors and *n* incomplete expressions

SAVING A SESSION

TRANSCRIPT

```
format:  (transcript optional-file-name-string)
```

The transcript function is useful as a learning aid, since it allows you to record an interactive session with the interpreter. When you execute this command, a file is opened and all the prompts and responses are written to this file. You can close the file within a session by calling the transcript function without a file name string. Exiting the interpreter automatically closes the currently opened file.

```
> (transcript "session1.doc")
T
•                         ;all commands will be saved
•                         ;to the file session1.doc
•
> (transcript)    ;close the file session1.doc
NIL
> (transcript "session2.doc")
T
•                         ;all commands will be saved
•                         ;to the file session2.doc
•
> (exit)          ;exiting the interpreter will also
                          ;close the current opened transcript file
```

2

Quick Start

This chapter provides a quick introduction to XLISP. Experienced programmers may find that enough information is presented here so that they can use the remainder of this text as a reference. Novices are exposed to the basic building blocks of the LISP language. The chapters to follow present in greater detail all of the information presented here.

We skip many of the syntax details and formal definitions of the language here. They are presented later. Once you gain confidence in writing simple programs in LISP, the more complex examples presented later will be easier to understand.

The examples presented here involve simple numeric processing, concepts that you are familiar with from everyday life. We examine the assign statement, some arithmetic functions, numeric predicates, a simple conditional, and an iterative construct.

Start the intepreter and enter the examples as you read the text. You can enter anything in boldface. Anything that follows the semicolon on a line is interpreted as a comment. Comments are not recognized by the XLISP interpreter, and you need not enter them.

ASSIGN STATEMENT

```
>  (setf  a  1)        ;SETF assigns the value 1 to a
1
>  (setf  b  2)        ;SETF assigns the value 2 to b
2

>  (setf  c  10)       ;SETF assigns the value 10 to c
10

>  a                   ;typing the name returns the value
1

>  b                   ;typing the name returns the value
2

>  c                   ;typing the name returns the value
10
```

ARITHMETIC FUNCTIONS

```
>  (+  1  2  3)                 ;addition
6

>  (+  a  b  c)                 ;remember,  a = 1,   b = 2,  c = 10
13

>  (*  4  5)                    ;multiplication
20

>  (/  20  5)                   ;division
4

>  (-  10  2)                   ;subtraction
8

>  (max  102  3)                ;return the larger number
102

>  (max  a  b  c)               ;return the largest number
10

>  (rem  10  3)                 ;remainder of 10/3 is 1
1
```

```
> (/ (+ 2 3 4) 3)              ;evaluate inner forms first
                               ;(/ 9 3) evaluates to 3
3

> (/ (+ a b c) 3)             ;same as above example
                               ;using a, b, and c
4

> (setf x (/ (+ a b c) 3))    ;initialize x
4
```

EXERCISES

Write expressions that will

1. Return the square of *b*.
2. Return the sum of the squares of *a*, *b*, and *c*.
3. Initialize *y* to the sum of the squares of *a*, *b*, and *c*.

ESTABLISHING A FUNCTION DEFINITION

The procedure DEFUN allows you to establish your own user-defined functions. Some simple examples are as follows:

```
> (defun GREETME ()           ;the empty () signify that no
                               ;arguments are passed
1> (print 'HOWDY)             ;PRINT displays information to you
1>)                            ;end function definition
                               ;returns the name
GREETME
```

You probably wondered why there was a quote mark preceding the HOWDY. If we want the name HOWDY printed, and not the value of HOWDY, the quote must be used. (In this instance, HOWDY does not have a value, since we never assigned one using SETF. An error would be generated if the name HOWDY was not quoted.) This is explained in detail later.

```
> (GREETME)          ;call the new function
HOWDY
HOWDY
```

The name HOWDY was returned twice. The PRINT function returned the name to you the first time. The XLISP interpreter returned HOWDY the second time, since any function executed by the interpreter always returns the value of the last statement executed.

The next example takes three integer arguments, sums them, and divides by three, returning the average of the three values.

```
> (defun AVERAGE (x y z)      ; 3 arguments passed
1> (/ (+ x y z) 3)            ; sum arguments and divide b y 3
1>)                           ; end function definition
AVERAGE

> (AVERAGE 1 2 3)
2

> (AVERAGE 67 88 94)
83

> (AVERAGE a b c)             ; a = 1, b = 2, c ; oe 10
4
```

EXERCISES

4. Write the function SUMSQUARE that takes three arguments and returns the sum of the squares. Try calling SUMSQUARE with the following arguments:

```
> (SUMSQUARE a b c)          ; a = 1, b =  2, c = 10
105
> (SUMSQUARE 1 2 3)
14
```

5. Write the function VOLUME that takes three arguments (length, width, and height of a box) and returns the volume of the box. Try calling VOLUME with the following arguments:

```
> (VOLUME 10 10 10)
1000

> (VOLUME 10 20 30)
6000
```

PREDICATES

Predicates return true (T) or false (NIL). They are used to test for certain conditions.

```
> (< 1 2)                    ; less than
T
```

```
> (> 4 2)                        ;greater than
T

> (> 10 20)
NIL

> ( = (* 2 3) (+ 3 3))           ;nested expressions
T

> (oddp 1)                       ;1 is an odd number
T

> (oddp 2)                       ;2 is not an odd number
NIL
```

We can write our own predicates. The following function returns true or false. If the multiplication of the first two arguments equals the multiplication of the last two, the function returns true; otherwise NIL (false) is returned.

```
> (defun MULTCOMPARE (w x y z)
1> (=
2>          (* w x)             ;multiply first two arguments
2>          (* y z)             ;multiply last two arguments
2> )                            ;close equality test
1> )                            ;end function definition
MULTCOMPARE

> (MULTCOMPARE 2 6 3 4)         ;2*6 equal 3*4
T

> (MULTCOMPARE 2 7 3 5)         ;2*7 not equal 3*5
NIL
```

EXERCISES

6. Write the predicate function BIG-ENUF that takes the length, height, and width of a box as arguments. If the total cubic feet is greater than 100, return T (true) or else return NIL (false). Try calling BIG-ENUF with the following arguments:

```
> (BIG-ENUF 10 10 10)
T

> (BIG-ENUF 2 2 2)
NIL
```

7. Write the predicate function GOES-INTO that takes two arguments. If the first argument is divisible by the second with no remainder, it will return T (true). Otherwise, it will return NIL (false). [Hint: Use the built-in remainder (REM) function.] Try calling GOES-INTO with the following arguments:

```
> (GOES-INTO 20 5)
T

> (GOES-INTO 20 6)
NIL
```

CONDITIONALS

The built-in function MAX returns the largest value of its arguments. We can write a new definition of MAX using the conditional IF test. The IF is similar to the if-then-else construct in other programming languages.

```
>  (defun X-MAX (a b)
1>     (if
2>          (> a b)           ; if a > b
2>          a                 ; return a
2>          b)                ; else return b
1>)                           ; end function definition
X-MAX

>  (X-MAX 2 3)
3

>  (X-MAX 3 2)
3

>  (X-MAX 100 8)
100
```

EXERCISES

Remember to use the quote to prevent evaluation of names.

8. Assume that you have 1 gallon of paint that will cover 400 square feet of wall. Write the function PAINT that takes the length, height, and width of a room, and calculates the square footage. It will print NEED-PAINT if the square footage is greater than 400 square feet. Otherwise, it will print HAVE-PAINT. Try calling PAINT with the following arguments:

```
> (PAINT 12 8 13)
HAVE-PAINT
HAVE-PAINT

> (PAINT 20 10 20)
NEED-PAINT
NEED-PAINT
```

9. Write the function PENNIES that takes as its argument an amount of change. It will return the amount of change left after you exchange all your coins for dollar bills. If there is no change, print NO-CHANGE. Try calling PENNIES with the following arguments:

(defun pennies (x)
(if

```
> (PENNIES 105)
5

> (PENNIES 1500)
NO-CHANGE
NO-CHANGE
```

10. Use the function GOES-INTO defined above to rewrite the function in Exercise 9.

Example

1. Given the information already presented, we can solve the following word problem: Write a function that calculates the payment on a house in the city of Boston. The mortgage payment on a $100,000 mortgage (at 9½ percent for 30 years) is $841. For each additional $1000 over $100,000, add $8.41. The formula is

$$\text{payment} = 841.00 + 8.41 * ((\text{mortgage} - 100000)/1000)$$

Translating this formula into a LISP expression, we obtain

```
(+ 841.00 (* 8.41 (/ (- mortgage 100000) 1000)))
```

We can now define a function:

```
> (defun CITY-RATE (mortgage)
1>     (+ 841.00 (* 8.41 (/ (- mortgage 100000) 1000)))
1>)
CITY-RATE
> (CITY-RATE 100000)
841.00

> (CITY-RATE 110000)
925.10

> (CITY-RATE 120000)
1009.20
```

Let's write a higher level function that first verifies that the amount to be mortgaged is actually greater than or equal to $100,000:

```
> (defun PAYMENT (mortgage)
1>    (if (>= mortgage 100000)      ;test
2>        (CITY-RATE mortgage)      ;true
2>        'INVALID-ENTRY)           ;else error message
1>)
PAYMENT

> (PAYMENT 100000)
841.00

> (PAYMENT 90000)
INVALID-ENTRY
```

EXERCISES

11. Write the function SUBURB-RATE that calculates the payment on a home between $50,000 and $100,000 using the formula

$$\text{payment} = \$370.00 + \$7.40 * (\text{mortgage} - 50000)/1000$$

Try calling SUBURB-RATE with the following arguments:

```
> (SUBURB-RATE 50000)
370.00

> (SUBURB-RATE 55000)
407.00

> (SUBURB-RATE 90000)
666.00
```

12. Rewrite the function PAYMENT so that it calls the new calculation SUBURB-RATE instead of generating an error message.

LISTS

Let's take another look at the integer-averaging problem.

```
(defun AVERAGE (x y z)
     (/ (+ x y z) 3))
```

Notice that the function takes three arguments and returns the average of the three numbers. What if we wanted to average 4 numbers, or six numbers, or 100 numbers? We could write many separate functions that would have an argument for each number. This quickly becomes quite cumbersome.

In LISP, however, we have the list data type. We can group together numbers on a list, and built-in functions in the LISP interpreter allow us to process a list of numbers of indefinite length. A list of numbers is grouped together with left and right parentheses. The following are examples of lists of numbers:

(1 2 3 4)
(90 100 400 200 540 27)

A list can be passed to a function as a single argument, even though the length of the list may vary each time the function is called. The built-in function LENGTH returns the number of elements on a list. Note that the list must be quoted. Remember, this is explained in detail later.

```
> (length '(1 2 3 4))
4

> (length '(90 100 400 200 540 27))
6

> (setf L '(1 2 3 4 5 6 7 8 9 10))    ;assign L the list of num bers
(1 2 3 4 5 6 7 8 9 10)

> (length L)                          ;return the number of ite ms
10                                    ;on the list
```

A SIMPLE ITERATIVE CONSTRUCT

DOLIST is a very simple iterative construct that processes each number on the list and terminates when it reaches the end.

does not show enough

```
(dolist (num L total)      ;establish initializations
                           ;for loop
(setf total (+ total num)))  ;add numbers in body of loop
```

Each time the loop is executed, the value of "num" is set to the value of each succeeding element on L. When all elements have been processed, the value "total" is returned. The body of the loop does the calculation.

We can define a function ADD-LIST that adds up each element on a list and returns the total:

```
(defun ADD-LIST (L &aux total)
    (setf total 0)
    (dolist (num L total)
        (setf total (+ total num)))))
```

Note the use of the auxiliary keyword in the argument list. Any parameters follow-ing this keyword are not passed as arguments, but are used internally within the function. The auxiliary parameter is similar to a local variable in PASCAL or C. In this example, the auxiliary parameter "total" is used to hold the sum of the list of numbers.

Putting it all together, we can redefine AVERAGE. The variable "total" is divided by the length of the list before returning the value. This gives us the average.

```
>  (defun AVERAGE (L &aux total)
1>  (setf total 0)
1>  (dolist (num L (/ total (length L)))  ;return average
2>         (setf total (+ total num))       ;sum up the list
2>  )
1>)
AVERAGE


>  L                                    ;remember value of L
(1 2 3 4 5 6 7 8 9 10)


>  (AVERAGE L)                          ;pass L as argument
5


>  (AVERAGE '(10 20 30 50)              ;pass lists of indefinite   lengths
27


>  (AVERAGE '(30))
30
```

EXERCISES

13. Rewrite AVERAGE to print the subtotal values computed during the iterative process. Try the function with the following arguments:

```
>  (AVERAGE '(10 20 30))
10
30
60
20
```

```
>  (AVERAGE  '(1  2  3  4))
1
3
6
10
2
```

14. Write a function SUMSQUARE similar to AVERAGE that returns the sum of the squares of the elements on a list. Try SUMSQUARE with the following arguments:

```
>  (SUMSQUARE  '(10  20  30))
1400
```

15. Using DOLIST, write the predicate function EVEN-NUMS that returns T (true) if all the numbers on a list are even. Otherwise it will return NIL (false) if any of the numbers are odd. Try EVEN-NUMS with the following arguments:

```
>  (EVEN-NUMS  '(2  4  8  10))
T

>  (EVEN-NUMS  '(2  4  8  11))
NIL
```

SUMMARY

At this point, you should be able to write simple expressions and function definitions. You should begin to feel comfortable with the LISP programming style and interacting with the interpreter. You have been exposed to some of the syntax of LISP in this quick introduction. The rest of this manual presents the language in greater detail.

ANSWERS

1. (* b b)

2. (+ (* a a) (* b b) (* c c))

3. (setf y (+ (* a a) (* b b) (* c c)))

4. (defun SUMSQUARE (x y z)
       (+ (* x x) (* y y) (* z z)))

5. (defun VOLUME (length width height)
       (* length width height))

6. (defun BIG-ENUF (length width height)
       (> (* length width height) 100))

```
7. (defun GOES-INTO (a b)
   (= 0 (rem a b))))
8. (defun PAINT (length width height)
     (if (> (* (* 2 (+ length width)) height) 400)
         (print 'NEED-PAINT) (print 'HAVE-PAINT)))
9. (defun PENNIES (coins)
     (if (= 0 (rem coins 100)) (print 'NO-CHANGE)
                               (rem coins 100)))
10. (defun PENNIES (coins)
      (if (GOES-INTO coins 100) (print 'NO-CHANGE)
                                (rem coins 100)))
11. (defun SUBURB-RATE (mortgage)
        (+ 370.00 (* 7.40 (/ (- mortgage 50000) 1000)))))
12. (defun PAYMENT (mortgage)
        (if (>= mortgage 100000)
            (CITY-RATE mortgage)
            (SUBURB-RATE mortgage)))
13. (defun AVERAGE (L &aux total)
      (setf total 0)
      (dolist (num L (/ total (length L)))      ;return average
          (setf total (+ total num))            ;sum up the list
          (print total)))
14. (defun SUMSQUARES (L &aux total)
      (setf total 0)
      (dolist (num L total)                            ;return sum of
          (setf total (+ total (* num num))))))       ;squares
15. (defun EVEN-NUMS (L &aux check)
      (setf check T)
      (dolist (num L check)
            (if (oddp num) (setf check NIL))))
```

3

Data Types

This chapter establishes definitions for the data types that are used throughout this book. A complete list of all the data types available in XLISP can be found in Appendix A.

SYMBOLS

A *symbol* is a LISP data object. Examples of valid symbols are

ABC
abc
value1
param-value
car
abcdefghijk
+
*

A valid symbol consists of any sequence of nonblank, printable characters except the following:

$$( ) ' @ , " ;$$

Upper- and lower-case characters are interpreted as being the same character. In the example above, the symbols *abc* and *ABC* are the same symbol. Symbol names can consist of up to 100 characters.

NUMBERS

Numbers can be integer literals or floating point numbers. These may be preceded by a "+" or "−" to indicate positive or negative. The range of values an integer or a float can represent depends upon the machine where XLISP is running. (For example, the IBM PC will allow integers in the range of −2,147,483,648 through +2,147,483,647.)

LISTS

A *list* is any expression beginning with a left parenthesis and ending with a right parenthesis. (Remember that a list must be a complete expression consisting of a matched number of left and right parentheses.) Lists can contain symbols, integers, strings, and other lists. Anything contained in a list is referred to as an *element* of the list. The following are examples of lists:

```
( )
(a b c d e f g)
((day 1)(hours 24)(minutes 1440))
("apples" "oranges" "bananas")
(+ 2 3)
```

STRINGS

String constants are sequences of characters surrounded by double quotes. A string constant can contain up to 100 characters. A single character is denoted as a string consisting of one character. The empty string " "(double quotes with no characters) is a valid string constant.

The backslash character \ is used to allow nonprintable characters to be included within a string. (Use \\ to represent a backslash. For example, "\\a" prints as \a.) The following are recognized within a string:

\\	the character \
\n	newline
\t	tab
\r	return
\f	formfeed
\nnn	character whose octal code is nnn

The following are examples of valid strings:

"m"
"abc"
"12345"
"This line will be followed by a newline. \n"

If you are entering a string and do not surround it with matching double quotes at the beginning and the end, the interpreter will not be able to recognize where to end the string. The interpreter will accept all subsequent keystrokes as characters on the string, and the initial prompt will not be returned to you. You must at this point enter the closing double quote, exit back up to top-level if an error has been generated, and retype the string, remembering to place the double quotes in the proper place.

ARRAYS

An *array* is a data structure with an assigned number of places. In XLISP, only one-dimensional arrays are allowed. The length of the array is initialized to an integer value. (The data type string described above is essentially a one-dimensional array of string characters.)

TRUE AND FALSE

Two special symbols that you will encounter are the symbol T (true) and the symbol NIL (false). These expressions are used to denote the results of a Boolean test. Any expression which evaluates to NIL is considered false. The empty list (), that is, a list with no elements, evaluates to NIL. Therefore, the empty list is considered false.

Any expression that returns a value other than NIL is considered true. The symbol T can be used as a default when we want to force an evaluation to true. The use of nonNIL to signal true becomes important when evaluating functions that return NIL if false or some useful value if not false.

SUBRS/FSUBRS*

XLISP has many built-in procedures. Procedures that evaluate their arguments and return a value are known as SUBRS or *functions*. Throughout the rest of this book, the Common LISP term *function* will be used to denote SUBRS. The arithmetic functions + and − are examples of functions that evaluate their arguments and return a value.

Some examples of procedures referred to as FSUBRS are those that may not evaluate all their arguments (such as Boolean AND and OR), or those that produce side effects (such as SETF, SETQ, DEFUN). Common LISP calls these procedures special forms, and some implementations of Common LISP further subdivide special forms into special forms and macros. This book uses the term *special form* to denote these procedures.

At this time, it is only necessary to be aware that there are two different types of procedures in LISP, and the distinction will become clearer as you become more familiar with the language.

FORMS

In order to utilize functions and special forms in LISP, they must appear as the first element on a list. The list (+ 2 3) is a function call that adds together the numbers 2 and 3. A list whose first element is a function or special form and whose succeeding elements are its arguments is an example of a *form*.

Arguments are evaluated from left to right, and the function is then applied to the results. Note: Anything that follows the character ; on a line is interpreted as a comment.

```
>  (+ 2 3)        ; add 2 and 3
5
```

If a form is used within another form, the innermost form is evaluated first, and the result is used within the outer form.

```
>  (+ 16 (+ 2 3))       ; is evaluated as (+ 16 5)
21
```

In a series of forms, arguments are evaluated from left to right, and the function is then applied to the results. The following example shows the order of evaluation:

```
>  ( + (+ 2 3)  (− 7 (− 8 2)))
;  (+ 5 (− 7 (− 8 2)))
;  (+ 5 (− 7 6))
;  (+ 5 1)
6

>
```

*Novices can skip this section.

If the first element of a form is not a function or special form, an error is generated. In this example, the symbol *a* is not a valid function:

```
>  (a  b  c)
error - unbound variable -A
if continued - try evaluating symbol again

1:>  (clean-up)
[abort to previous level]

>
```

We discuss a way to inhibit the evaluation of elements on a list in the next chapter.

4

Some Built-In Procedures

In this chapter, you are introduced to some built-in LISP procedures. A *built-in procedure* is any procedure supplied by the LISP interpreter itself, rather than one that has been defined by the user.

Throughout the following chapters, the general format of the procedure follows the procedure name. You are encouraged to start the interpreter and enter the examples as you encounter them. (Remember, **boldface** indicates expressions you can enter into the computer.) Exercises are at the end of the chapter.

ASSIGNMENT FUNCTIONS

SETQ

```
format: (setq symbol value)
```

The value of a symbol is initialized using the special form SETQ. (SETQ is like the assignment statement in BASIC.) The first argument must be a symbol, which will be assigned the value of the second argument. The symbol's value is displayed by entering the symbol name. Try entering the following sequence of expressions:

```
> (setq a 1)              ; the symbol a is set to  1
1

> a                       ; get the value of a
1

> (setq b 2 c 3)          ; initializing multiple symbols
                          ; only the last value is returned
3

> b                       ; get the value of b
2

> c                       ; get the value of c
3

> (+ a b c)               ; the value of each symbol added together
6

> A                       ; note that lower- and upper-case symbol
                          ; names are equivalent
1

> B
2

> C
3
```

SETF

format: (setf symbol value)

The special form SETF is also used to initialize the value of a symbol, exactly the same as SETQ. Either special form is correct. SETF is also used to initialize values of other data types with fields, such as list nodes, arrays, properties, and so forth. For now, you only need to know that SETF is equivalent to SETQ when initializing symbol values. The other uses are described as they are needed.

```
> (setf x 99)
99

> x
99
```

SUPPRESSING EVALUATION

QUOTE

```
format: (quote arg) or 'arg
```

The QUOTE special form suppresses evaluation. When the interpreter is handed a list to evaluate, it evaluates the first element on the list and applies it to the rest of the list. This is fine if the list is also a form, in which case the first element on the list is a function or special form. Remember the form (+ a b) applies the LISP function + to add two numbers together.

Sometimes, however, we want to generate a list of elements whose first element is not a procedure. For example, we might want a list of names or numbers. We need a method of suppressing evaluation of the first element. The QUOTE procedure (which is equivalent to the character ') accomplishes this.

Examples

```
> (a b c)              ; an unquoted list is treated as a form
                       ; a is not a defined function
                       ; this form generates an error
error: bad function - (A B C)

1:> (clean-up)>        ; return to top-level of interpreter
(abort to previous level)

> (quote (a b c))      ; quoting returns list without evaluation
(A B C)

> '(a b c)             ; the character ' is shorthand for quote
(A B C)

> '(+ 2 3)             ; quoting a form returns the form
                       ; unevaluated, the addition function is not
                       ; applied to its arguments

(+ 2 3)
```

ARITHMETIC FUNCTIONS

The arithmetic functions evaluate their arguments, which must be either integer or floating point numbers, and return a value. They take an unlimited number of arguments except as noted above. Enter the following sequence of forms, noting the order of evaluation.

Function	Description	Format
+	addition	(+ arg⊥ . . . argn)
−	subtraction	(− arg⊥ . . . argn)
*	multiplication	(* arg⊥ . . . argn)
/	division	(1 arg⊥ . . . argn)
1 +	increment by 1	(1 + arg)
1 −	decrement by 1	(1 − arg)
REM	remainder	(rem arg1 . . . argn)
MIN	minimum value	(min arg1 . . . argn)
MAX	maximum value	(max arg1 . . . argn)
ABS	absolute value	(abs arg)
TRUNCATE	convert floating point number to integer	(truncate arg)
FLOAT	convert integer to floating point number	(float arg)

Examples

```
> (− 100 50 40)              ; 100 − 50 =  50, then 50 − 40 = 10
10

> (− 0 90)
−90

> (− 90)                     ; this is a special case  which is
                             ; evaluated the same as the above
                             ; example (− 0 90)
−90

> (/ 10 3)
3

> (/ 20 4 5)                 ; 20/4 = 5, then 5/5  = 1
1

> (/ 99.9 3)
33.3000

> (rem 10 3)
1

> (rem 20 3)
2

> (1+ 10)                    ; increment by 1
11

> (1− 10)                    ; decrement by 1
9
```

```
> (abs −1000)
1000

> (min 100 50 25)
25

> (max 100 50 25)
100

> (truncate 3.1416)
3

> (float 89)
89.0000

> (setf a (min 110 100 50))
50

> (setf a (/ a 2))
25

> (setf a (* 20 a))
500
```

The three forms described above could be combined as follows to generate the same answer:

```
> (setf a (* 20 (/ (min 110 100 50) 2)))
500
```

STRING FUNCTIONS

Function	Description
STRCAT	concatenate strings
SUBSTR	extract a substring
LENGTH	compute string length
CHAR	extract a character from a string
STRING	make a string from an integer ASCII value

The character string data type consists of a sequence of characters between double quotes. Characters within a string are treated exactly as they appear; lower- and upper-case characters are distinct. The string functions are useful when writing to and reading from a text file, as well as printing messages to your terminal from within user-defined procedures. (These functions are not strictly compatible with the character sequence functions in Common LISP as described by Guy Steele in *Common LISP*.*)

*Guy L. Steele, Jr., *Common LISP* (Burlington, MA., Digital Press, 1984).

STRCAT

```
format: (strcat string-elt1 . . . string-eltn)
```

The STRCAT function will concatenate an unlimited number of strings.

```
> (setf s1 "string")              ; initialize the string s1
"string"

> (setf s2 "i am a ")             ; initialize the string s2
"i am a "

> (strcat s2 s1)                  ; concatenate strings s2 and s1
"i am a string"

> (setf s3 (strcat s2 s1))        ; initialize s3 to merge of s2 and s1
"i am a string"
```

SUBSTR

```
format: (substr string-elt start optional-length)
```

The SUBSTR function returns a substring of a given string element. The start position is specified by an integer value. The optional length integer is the length of the string to be extracted. This argument is optional and defaults to the rest of the string.

```
> s3
"i am a string"
> (substr s3 1 1)        ; return first character of string
"i"
> (substr s3 8)          ; return characters 8 through end of string
"string"
```

LENGTH

```
format: (length string-elt)
```

The length function computes the number of characters on a string and returns that value.

```
> (length s3)            ; return length of ""i am a string"
13

> (length "")            ; empty string
0
```

The following functions are useful for converting data from string data to equivalent ASCII codes or numeric data, and vice versa. The ASCII code is the internal numeric code used to represent the character. There is an ASCII code for each letter of the alphabet, both upper- and lower-case; numbers; and most commonly used punctuation marks.

CHAR

format: (char string-elt index)

The CHAR function converts a character on a string to its numeric ASCII code. The index is zero-relative and determines which character to convert. *"Zero-relative"* means that the first character on the string is indexed by the integer 0 and the *n*th character on the string is indexed by $n - 1$.

```
> (char "k" 0)          ; ASCII equivalent of lowercase "k"
107

> (char "zebra" 2)      ; ASCII equivalent of lower-case "b"
98
```

STRING

format: (string expr)

The STRING function converts a valid ASCII code to its character equivalent and returns a one-character string.

```
> (string 107)        ; return character equivalent of 107
"k"

> (string 98)
"b"
```

EXERCISES

Evaluate the following expressions:

1. (+ (1+ 100) (abs −1))
2. (float (truncate 6.87))
3. (min (rem 10 6) (/ 12 4))
4. (/ (+ 10 20 30) 2)
5. (+ (* 100 (abs (− 100 105))) −500)

Initialize the following string: (setf name "John Doe"). Write expressions that will

6. Return the number of characters in the string.
7. Return the first character of the first name.
8. Return the last name.
9. Return the first character of the last name.
10. Return the numeric ASCII equivalent of the first character of the last name.
11. Concatenate the phone number "555-1212" onto the name.

ANSWERS

1. 102
2. 6.0000
3. 3
4. 30
5. 0
6. (length name)
7. (substr name 1 1)
8. (substr name 6)
9. (substr name 6 1)
10. (char (substr name 6 1) 0)
11. (strcat name "555-1212")

5

User-Defined Functions

The procedures you have been evaluating up to this point have all been provided by the system. In order to define your own procedures, the procedure *defun* is provided. It allows you to create your own definitions for complex expressions that you may want to use many times, but do not want to have to continually enter into the computer. DEFUN is a special form, a procedure that does not evaluate its arguments. It only establishes a definition and returns to you the procedure name.

DEFINING PROCEDURES

DEFUN (Defining a Procedure without Arguments)

```
                    format: (defun symbol () <body>)
```

```
> (defun HELLO () (print 'GREETINGS))      ; establish definition
                                           ; returns name of procedure
HELLO
```

The procedure name is returned, which tells you that the procedure definition has been established. This name can now be used as the first element on a form to be evaluated. In the example above, the empty list following the procedure name indicates that the procedure is not expecting any arguments. An association has been created between the name HELLO and the expressions necessary to print the symbol GREETINGS. (A detailed description of the PRINT procedure is presented in Chapter 16.) The procedure returns the value of the last statement executed. You can now call your new routine by specifying the new procedure name as the first argument on a form:

```
> (HELLO)          ; execute procedure
GREETINGS
GREETINGS
```

Notice that the symbol GREETINGS is returned to you twice. The first GREETINGS is a result of the PRINT statement within the procedure, displaying its argument to your terminal (standard output). The second occurrence appears because the procedure returns the value of the last statement executed, in this case the result of the PRINT statement again. If you wanted to avoid the double display of GREETINGS to your terminal, you can insert a NIL as the last statement in the function:

```
> (defun HELLO () (print 'GREETINGS) NIL)
HELLO

> (HELLO)
GREETINGS
NIL
```

DEFUN (Defining a Procedure with Arguments)

```
format: (defun symbol (arg1 . . . argn) <body>)
```

A procedure definition can be established to allow the new procedure to accept arguments. These are formal arguments that the caller of the procedure must supply, or an error is generated. In these examples we can use the arithmetic functions we know about to define our own procedures.

Examples

1. This procedure will return the square of a number.

```
> (defun SQUARE (x)       ; x is a formal argument
1> (* x x))               ; body of function
SQUARE

> (SQUARE 9)              ; calling the function requires a
                          ; numeric argument
```

2. This procedure is used to convert inches to centimeters.

```
> (defun CENTIM (inch)
1> (* inch 2.54))
CENTIM

> (CENTIM 15.0)
38.1000

> (CENTIM 32.5)
82.5500
```

3. This procedure returns total value of coins.

```
> (defun CHANGE (pennies nickels dimes quarters)
1> (+ pennies (* nickels 5) (* dimes 10) (* quarters 25)))
CHANGE

; 4 pennies + 2 nickels + 3 dimes + 2 quarters = $.94

> (CHANGE 4 2 3 2)
94

; 1 penny + 6 nickels + 0 dimes + 7 quarters = $2.06

> (CHANGE 1 6 0 7)
206
```

DEFUN (Defining a Function with Optional Arguments)

```
format: (defun symbol (arg1 . . . argn &optional arg1 . . . argn)
         <body>)
```

You can also indicate to the function that there may be optional arguments passed to it with the &optional parameter. If the optional argument is not present, the symbol will be initialized to NIL when the function is invoked.

```
> (defun ASSIGN-A (&optional val)
1> (setf a val))
ASSIGN-A

> (ASSIGN-A)
NIL

> a
NIL
```

```
>  (ASSIGN-A 10)
10


>  a
10
```

DEFUN (Defining a Function with Auxiliary Arguments)

```
format:  (defun symbol (arg1 . . . argn &optional arg1 . . . argn
                                     &aux arg1 . . . argn)

      <body>)
```

Variables that you will use internally within the function that have no effect on the outside environment are listed after the &aux parameter. In many cases, the use of these temporary intermediate variables makes a procedure easier to read and understand by allowing you to break calculations into manageable parts.

```
>  (defun RANGE (x y z &aux min-value max-value)
1> (setf min-value (min x y z))
1> (setf max-value (max x y z))
1> (- max-value min-value))
RANGE                                    ; returns name


>  (RANGE 100 30 40)
70


>  (RANGE 4 2 20)
18
```

FREE AND BOUND VARIABLES

There are many subtleties in LISP regarding the use of bound and free variables. As a beginner, you should always avoid the use of free variables. A *free variable* is a symbol that does not appear in the procedure's parameter list. See the example ASSIGN-A above, in which *a* was a free variable. The symbols you use within your user-defined functions should always be bound, that is, passed as an argument to the function. If you need to use temporary symbols within your routine, they should be listed as auxiliary parameters. This attention to detail will help you avoid errors that are difficult to debug.

LOADING USER-DEFINED FUNCTIONS

The functions you have been entering into the system so far have been concise. If you want to create a sizable function with many statements, it would be cumbersome to enter each statement every time you started the interpreter. It would be more convenient if you could enter the function statements into a file that the XLISP interpreter could then read. The function LOAD allows you to load functions that have been defined in a source file. These XLISP source files must have ''.lsp'' appended to them. In this manner, you can create libraries of routines that you can initialize when you start the program.

LOAD

format: (load file-name-string)

Create the file math.lsp with your editor and enter the statements to create the function SQUARE from above. Close the file and start the interpreter.

```
> (SQUARE 10)                    ; SQUARE is not a valid function
error - unbound variable - SQUARE

1:> (clean-up)
[abort to previous level]

> (load "math")                  ; load the file containing the definition
                                 ; of SQUARE
; loading "math.lsp"
T                                ; returns T if successful

> (boundp 'SQUARE)               ; SQUARE is now a valid function
T

> (SQUARE 9)                     ; try the function
81

>                                ; it works! no error!
```

LOADING USER-DEFINED FUNCTIONS AT INITIALIZATION

You can load your files when you start the interpreter if you specify the file names on the command line. Do not enter the names as strings when loading from the command line. The system assumes a file extension of ''.lsp'' to each file you specify. Therefore, all files you create with the editor containing XLISP functions should have a file extension of ''.lsp''. You could also have loaded your function SQUARE by specifying:

```
xlisp math
XLISP version 1.7, Copyright (c) 1986, by David Betz
; loading "math.lsp"

> (SQUARE 10)
100
```

Note that more than one user-defined function can be defined in your source file. Also, more than one source file can be specified when loading; separate each file name on the line with a space. You will obtain the following error at load time if the parentheses in your file do not match:

```
error: unexpected EOF
1:>
```

At this point, you must exit the interpreter and edit the file, correcting the error.

EDITING FROM WITHIN THE XLISP ENVIRONMENT

If you are running the interpreter on a DOS compatible machine, XLISP provides the function DOS, which allows you to execute operating system commands from within the XLISP environment. You can create or update, edit and save a file without exiting the interpreter. The argument to DOS must be the command string within double quotes. The editor EDLIN is used as an example:

```
> (dos "A:edlin B:sample.lsp")       ; EDLIN on drive A
                                      ; sample.lsp on drive B
```

[Use editor commands to enter or change text and save the file. Exiting the editor will return you to the interpreter.]

```
T                                     ; T is returned
> (load "B:sample")                   ; remember to reload your new or
                                      ; corrected file
; loading "sample.lsp"
T
```

EXERCISES

1. Write the procedure PERIMETER that takes the width and length of a rectangle as arguments and returns the perimeter.
2. Using the procedure CHANGE, write POCKET-CHANGE that returns the amount of change left after exchanging each whole dollar's worth of coins for dollar bills.
3. Write the procedure SUM-SQUARE that returns the sum of the squares of its two arguments.
4. Write CIRCUMFERENCE that takes the radius of a circle as its argument and returns the circumference of the circle.

ANSWERS

1. (defun PERIMETER (length width)
        (* 2 (+ length width)))

2. (defun POCKET-CHANGE (pennies nickels dimes quarters)
       (rem (CHANGE pennies nickels dimes quarters) 100))

3. (defun SUM-SQUARE (x y)
       (+ (* x x)(* y y)))
or (if the function SQUARE has been defined)
(defun SUM-SQUARE (x y)
       (+ (SQUARE x)(SQUARE y)))

4. (defun CIRCUMFERENCE (radius)
       (* 3.1416 (* radius radius)))
or (if the function SQUARE has been defined)
(defun CIRCUMFERENCE (radius)
       (* 3.1416 (SQUARE radius)))

6

Built-In Procedures for Creating Lists

Procedure	Description
LIST	create a list
CONS	add an element to the beginning of the list
APPEND	merge several lists into one list

Most of the lists we have been evaluating so far have been forms. The first element on the list has been a procedure followed by its arguments. Now we begin to look at the procedures that manipulate lists simply as collections of symbols.

CREATING A LIST

There are several functions we can use to create lists. If we know which elements are to be included on the list, we can initialize it using the LIST function. We can also add elements onto existing lists using the functions CONS and APPEND.

LIST

format: (list arg1 . . . argn)

The function LIST is used to create a list. The elements we want on the list are specified as arguments to the function. Symbol names and lists must be quoted to prevent evaluation. This function can take an unlimited number of arguments.

Examples

```
> (LIST 'APPLES 'PEARS)
(APPLES PEARS)

> (LIST 'A 'B 'C 1 2 3)
(A B C 1 2 3)

> (SETF FRUIT (LIST 'APPLES 24 'PEARS 12))
(APPLES 24 PEARS 12)

> FRUIT
(APPLES 24 PEARS 12)
```

CONS

format: (cons element list-expr)

The function CONS is used to construct a list by adding an element onto the front of the list. Note that CONS does not permanently alter the list expression.

Examples

```
> (CONS 1 '())                              ; CONSing onto the null list
(1)

> (CONS 1 '(2 3))
(1 2 3)

> (CONS 'BUSHELS FRUIT)
(BUSHELS APPLES 24 PEARS 12)

> (SETF ZOO (LIST 'BEARS 'MONKEYS))
(BEARS MONKEYS)

> (SETF CLEVE-ZOO (CONS 'ELEPHANT ZOO))
(ELEPHANT BEARS MONKEYS)

> ZOO                                       ; ZOO is unchanged
(BEARS MONKEYS)
```

APPEND

format: (append list-expr1 . . . list-exprn)

The function APPEND is used to add elements to a list by merging several lists together. All the arguments to this function must be lists. The function merges the lists and returns one list with all the elements.

Examples

> **(APPEND ' (1) ' (2 3))**
(1 2 3)

> **(APPEND ' (1) ' ( ))**
(1)

> **(APPEND ' (BERRIES 100) FRUIT)**
(BERRIES 100 APPLES 24 PEARS 12)

> **(SETF WASH-ZOO (LIST 'PANDAS 'CAMELS))**
(PANDAS CAMELS)

> **(SETF ZOO-ANIMALS (APPEND WASH-ZOO CLEVE-ZOO))**
(PANDAS CAMELS ELEPHANT BEARS MONKEYS)

> **CLEVE-ZOO**
(ELEPHANT BEARS MONKEYS)

> **WASH-ZOO**
(PANDAS CAMELS)

> **ZOO-ANIMALS**
(PANDAS CAMELS ELEPHANT BEARS MONKEYS)

EXERCISES

Evaluate the following, assuming the values have been set as above:

1. (CONS WASH-ZOO CLEVE-ZOO)
2. (LIST WASH-ZOO CLEVE-ZOO)
3. (CONS 'ANIMALS (LIST WASH-ZOO CLEVE-ZOO))
4. (LIST (CONS 'ANIMALS WASH-ZOO)
           (CONS 'ANIMALS CLEVE-ZOO))

5. (APPEND '(ANIMALS) WASH-ZOO CLEVE-ZOO)

(SETF JEWELS '(RUBIES EMERALDS) COLORS '(RED GREEN))

6. (LIST JEWELS COLORS)
7. (CONS JEWELS COLORS)
8. (APPEND JEWELS COLORS)

ANSWERS

1. ((PANDAS CAMELS) ELEPHANT BEARS MONKEYS)
2. ((PANDAS CAMELS) (ELEPHANT BEARS MONKEYS))
3. (ANIMALS (PANDAS CAMELS) (ELEPHANT BEARS MONKEYS))
4. ((ANIMALS PANDAS CAMELS) (ANIMALS ELEPHANT BEARS MONK EYS))
5. (ANIMALS PANDAS CAMELS ELEPHANT BEARS MONKEYS)
6. ((RUBIES EMERALDS) (RED GREEN))
7. ((RUBIES EMERALDS) RED GREEN)
8. (RUBIES EMERALDS RED GREEN)

7

Built-In Procedures
for Manipulating Lists

Procedure	Description
CAR	return the first element of a list
CDR*	return the list with the first element discarded
LAST	return a list containing the last element of a list
NTHCDR	return the nth CDR of a list
NTH '	return the nth element of a list
Composition Functions	
CxxR:	all combinations as follows:
CAAR	(car (car list-expr))
CADR	(car (cdr list-expr))
CDAR	(cdr (car list-expr))
CDDR	(cdr (cdr list-expr))
CxxxR:	all combinations
CxxxxR:	all combinations

*CDR is pronounced either "cooder" or "kidder," depending on the area of the country where LISP is being taught.

MANIPULATING LIST EXPRESSIONS

Sometimes we want to take lists apart. We may want to know what the first element is on the list, or we may want to deal with an item nested within the list. The functions CAR and CDR allow us to manipulate list expressions. Note that while CAR returns a single *element*, CDR returns a list *expression*.

CAR

format: (car list-expr)

The function CAR returns the first element from a list. Its argument must be a list expression or an error will be generated. (Some Common LISP implementations call this function FIRST, which is more mnemonic.)

Examples

```
> (SETF FRUIT '(APPLES 24 PEARS 12))
(APPLES 24 PEARS 12)

> (CAR FRUIT)              ;return first element
APPLES

> (CAR '(A B C 1 2 3))
A

> (CAR '(LIST 1 2 3))
LIST
```

CDR

format (cdr list-expr)

The function CDR returns the list with the first element discarded. If the list is empty, the symbol NIL will be returned. Its argument must be a list expression or an error will be generated. (Some Common LISP implementations use the more mnemonic name REST for this function.)

Examples

```
> (CDR FRUIT)              ;return the list without the first element
(24 PEARS 12)

> (CDR '(A B C 1 2 3))
(B C 1 2 3)

> (CDR '(LIST 1 2 3))
(1 2 3)
```

LAST

format: (last list-expr)

The function LAST returns the last CONS of a list. It does not return the last element on a list, as might be expected, but a *list* containing the last element. If an empty list is specified, NIL will be returned.

Examples

> **(LAST FRUIT)**
(12)

> **(LAST '(1 2 3 97 98 99))**
(99)

> **(LAST '())**
NIL

NTHCDR

format: (nthcdr n list-expr)

The function NTHCDR returns the *n*th CDR of a list if *n* is an integer less than or equal to the length of the list. (The list is returned with the first *n* elements removed). If *n* is greater than the length of the list, NIL is returned. If $n = 0$, the original list is returned.

Examples

> **FRUIT**
(APPLES 24 PEARS 12)

> **(NTHCDR 0 FRUIT)**
(APPLES 24 PEARS 12)

> **(NTHCDR 1 FRUIT)**
(24 PEARS 12)

> **(NTHCDR 2 FRUIT)**
(PEARS 12)

> **(NTHCDR 3 FRUIT)**
(12)

> **(NTHCDR 4 FRUIT)**
NIL

NTH

```
format: (nth integer-expr list-expr)
```

The function NTH retrieves an element from a list. The integer value following the function specifies which element to return. (NTH does *n* CDR's on the list and returns the CAR of the resulting list.) NIL will be returned if this value is greater than the number of items on a list.

Examples

```
> (CAR (NTHCDR 0 FRUIT))        ; (APPLES 24 PEARS 12)
APPLES

> (NTH 0 FRUIT)                 ; 0 1 2 3
APPLES

> (NTH 1 FRUIT)
24

> (NTH 2 FRUIT)
PEARS

> (NTH 3 FRUIT)
12

> (NTH 4 FRUIT)
NIL
```

SETF

```
format (setf place value)
```

The special form SETF can be used to change the expressions on a list. The place specified as the first argument can be the CAR, CDR, or NTH position on the list expression. SETF permanently alters list expressions and should be used with caution.

Examples

```
> FRUIT
(APPLES 24 PEARS 12)

> (SETF (CAR FRUIT) 'MACINTOSH)
MACINTOSH

> FRUIT
(MACINTOSH 24 PEARS 12)

> (SETF (CDR FRUIT) '(16 GOLDEN-DEL 120))
(16 GOLDEN-DEL 120)
```

```
> FRUIT
(MACINTOSH 16 GOLDEN-DEL 120)

> (SETF (NTH 2 FRUIT) 'PEACHES)
PEACHES

> FRUIT
(MACINTOSH 16 PEACHES 120)
```

COMPOSITION FUNCTIONS

The following functions are a shorthand way to extract elements from nested lists. They are compositions of the CAR and CDR functions described above, often referred to as *CxR functions*. XLISP supports CxxR, CxxxR, and CxxxxR combinations, where each "x" represents an "A" for CAR or a "D" for CDR. The examples below demonstrate some of these functions.

Initialize the following list:

```
> (SETF VEGGIES (LIST '(CARROT ORANGE) '(TOMATO RED) '(PEA GREEN)))
((CARROT ORANGE) (TOMATO RED) (PEA GREEN))
```

CAAR

```
      format: (caar list-expr) is equivalent to (car (car list-expr))
```

Examples

```
> (CAR VEGGIES)
(CARROT ORANGE)

> (CAR (CAR VEGGIES))
CARROT

> (CAAR VEGGIES)
CARROT
```

CADR

```
      format (cadr list-expr) is equivalent to (car (cdr  list-expr))
```

Examples

```
> (CDR VEGGIES)
((TOMATO RED) (PEA GREEN))
```

> (CAR (CDR VEGGIES))
(TOMATO RED)

> (CADR VEGGIES)
(TOMATO RED)

CDAR

> format: (cdar list-expr) is equivalent to (cdr (car list-expr))

Examples

> (CAR VEGGIES)
(CARROT ORANGE)

> (CDR (CAR VEGGIES))
(ORANGE)

> (CDAR VEGGIES)
(ORANGE)

CDDR

> format: (cddr list-expr) is equivalent to (cdr (cdr list-expr))

Examples

> (CDR VEGGIES)
((TOMATO RED) (PEA GREEN))

> (CDR (CDR VEGGIES))
((PEA GREEN))

> (CDDR VEGGIES)
((PEA GREEN))

ARRAYS

An *array* is a data structure containing a fixed number of slots. In XLISP, MAKE-ARRAY creates a one-dimensional array. (A one-dimensional array is often called a *vector*.) The number of slots the array contains is initialized when it is created. The array slot numbers are referenced from 0.

When you type in the array name, the printed representation of the array appears on your terminal. For printing purposes, XLISP encloses the array within parentheses the same as the list data type, but precedes it by a # sign, which visually distinguishes it from a list.

Function	Description
MAKE-ARRAY	create an array
AREF	identifies a place in an array
SETF	initialize a value in an array
MAKE-ARRAY	format: (make-array integer-value)
AREF	format: (aref array slot-number)
SETF	format: (setf (aref array slot-number) value)

Examples

```
> (setf days-array (make-array 7))
#(NIL NIL NIL NIL NIL NIL NIL)

> (setf (aref days-array 1) 'monday)
MONDAY

> (aref days-array 1)
MONDAY

> (aref days-array 5)
NIL
> (setf (aref days-array 5) 'friday)
FRIDAY

> days-array
#(NIL MONDAY NIL NIL NIL FRIDAY NIL)

> (aref days-array 0)
NIL

> (setf (aref days-array 0) 'sunday)
SUNDAY

> days-array
#(SUNDAY MONDAY NIL NIL NIL FRIDAY NIL)
```

EXERCISES

Evaluate the following:

```
(SETF JEWELS '((RUBIES EMERALDS) (RED GREEN) (12 24)))
```

1. (CAR JEWELS)
2. (CDR JEWELS)
3. (CAR (CDR JEWELS))
4. (CDR (CAR JEWELS))
5. (CAADDR JEWELS)
6. (CDADR JEWELS)
7. (CAR (NTH 1 JEWELS))
8. (CAR (NTHCDR 1 JEWELS))
9. (CAR (LAST JEWELS))
10. (CDR (LAST JEWELS))
11. (LAST (CAR JEWELS))
12. (LAST (CDR JEWELS))
13. Write the procedures FIRST, SECOND, and THIRD which will return the first, second, or third element of a list using the composition functions.

ANSWERS

1. (RUBIES EMERALDS)
2. ((RED GREEN) (12 24))
3. (RED GREEN)
4. (EMERALDS)
5. 12
6. (GREEN)
7. RED
8. (RED GREEN)
9. (12 24)
10. NIL
11. (EMERALDS)
12. ((12 24))
13. (defun FIRST (L) (car L))
    (defun SECOND (L) (cadr L))
    (defun THIRD (L) (caddr L))

8

More List Functions

Procedure	Description
LENGTH	return the length of a list
REVERSE	reverse the elements on a list
REMOVE	remove an expression from a list
SUBST	substitute expressions
MEMBER	find an expression in a list

We have learned how to create list expressions and how to retrieve the elements of a list. The functions discussed in this chapter give us more information about lists or permit us to do additional operations on lists that we will find helpful.

HOW LONG IS A LIST?

LENGTH

```
format: (length list-expr)
```

LENGTH returns the number of top-level expressions on a list. The term *top-level* is discussed later in this chapter.

Examples

```
>  (LENGTH  '(1  2))
2

>  (LENGTH  '(ELT1  ELT2  ELT3  ELT4  ELT5))
5
```

REVERSING A LIST

REVERSE

format: (reverse list-expr)

The REVERSE function reverses the order of top-level elements on a list.

Examples

```
>  (SETF  ZOO-ANIMALS  '(PANDAS  CAMELS  ELEPHANT  BEARS  MONKEYS))
(PANDAS  CAMELS  ELEPHANT  BEARS  MONKEYS)

>  (REVERSE  ZOO-ANIMALS)
(MONKEYS  BEARS  ELEPHANT  CAMELS  PANDAS)

>  (SETF  BACKWARD-ZOO  (REVERSE  ZOO-ANIMALS))
(MONKEYS  BEARS  ELEPHANT  CAMELS  PANDAS)

>  ZOO-ANIMALS
(PANDAS  CAMELS  ELEPHANT  BEARS  MONKEYS)

>  BACKWARD-ZOO
(MONKEYS  BEARS  ELEPHANT  CAMELS  PANDAS)
```

MODIFYING LIST EXPRESSIONS

REMOVE

format: (remove expr list-expr)

The REMOVE function removes all occurrences of an expression from a list expression. The original list expression is unaltered. A copy of the list (with all occurrences of the specified element deleted) is returned to you.

Examples

```
>  (SETF  A  '(1  2  3  1  2  3))
(1  2  3  1  2  3)

>  (REMOVE  1  A)
(2  3  2  3)

>  A                               ;original list is unchanged
(1  2  3  1  2  3)

>  (SETF  B  (REMOVE  2  A))
(1  3  1  3)

>  B
(1  3  1  3)
```

SUBST

format: (subst new-expr old-expr list-expr)

The SUBST function substitutes all occurrences of an expression in a list with a new expression. The original list is unaltered. A copy of the list with the substitutions is returned to you.

Examples

```
>  (SETF  A  '(1  2  3  1  2  3  1  1))
(1  2  3  1  2  3  1  1)

>  (SUBST  'X  1  A)
(X  2  3  X  2  3  X  X)

>  A                               ;list A is unaltered
(1  2  3  1  2  3  1  1)

>  (SETF  B  (SUBST  'X  1  A))
(X  2  3  X  2  3  X  X)

>  B
(X  2  3  X  2  3  X  X)
```

QUERYING A LIST

MEMBER

format: (member expr list-expr)

The MEMBER function determines if a list contains a specified expression. If the expression is on the list, a list is returned containing all the elements including and following the test expression. If the expression is not present, NIL will be returned. The expression tested for is usually a symbol, number, file or string.

Examples

```
>  (SETF A '(BALLS BATS GLOVES))
(BALLS BATS GLOVES)

>  (MEMBER 'BALLS A)
(BALLS BATS GLOVES)

>  (MEMBER 'BATS A)
(BATS GLOVES)

>  (MEMBER 'GLOVES A)
(GLOVES)

>  (MEMBER 'SOCKS A)
NIL
```

PREDICATES

The function MEMBER can be considered an example of a predicate. A *predicate* is a function that returns a true or false value. When the MEMBER function returns a nonNIL value, it can be viewed as returning a value of ''true'' meaning the expression is on the list. (Remember, in LISP ''if it's not NIL, it's true.'') Predicates are discussed in detail in the next chapter.

TOP-LEVEL

Most of the examples given for the functions discussed above worked on the top-level elements of the lists. The *top-level elements* of a list are the elements that are not nested within sublists. A top-level element can contain nested expressions. The top-level elements are obtained using the CAR function applied to the list and applied to all CDR's of the list, as shown in the following example:

Example

```
>  (SETF BOOKS '(COURSES (MATH (TRIG GEOM)) (SCIENCE (CHEM BIOL))))
(COURSES (MATH (TRIG GEOM)) (SCIENCE (CHEM BIOL)))

>  (CAR BOOKS)
COURSES                             ;top-level element

>  (CAR (CDR BOOKS))
(MATH (TRIG GEOM))                  ;top-level element

>  (CAR (CDR (CDR BOOKS)))
(SCIENCE (CHEM BIOL))               ;top-level element
```

The functions LENGTH, REVERSE, REMOVE, and MEMBER are applied only
to top-level elements of a list. They do not recognize elements that are nested within list
expressions. SUBST will recognize elements that are nested and will dive into a list structure to replace individual expressions.

Examples

```
3 >  (LENGTH BOOKS)                     ;counts top-level element
>  (REVERSE BOOKS)                      ;reverse top-level elements
((SCIENCE (CHEM BIOL)) (MATH (TRIG GEOM)) COURSES)

>  (REMOVE 'GEOM BOOKS)                 ;not a top-level element
(COURSES (MATH (TRIG GEOM)) (SCIENCE (CHEM BIOL)))

>  (REMOVE 'GEOM (CAR (CDR (CAR (CDR BOOKS))))) ;this works
(TRIG)

>  (SUBST 'PSYCH 'CHEM BOOKS)          ;replace inside nested expressions
(COURSES (MATH (TRIG GEOM)) (SCIENCE (PSYCH BIOL)))

>  (MEMBER 'COURSES BOOKS)             ;top-level element
(COURSES (MATH (TRIG GEOM)) (SCIENCE (CHEM BIOL)))

>  (MEMBER 'TRIG BOOKS)                ;not a top-level element
NIL

>  (MEMBER 'TRIG (CADADR BOOKS))       ;this works
(TRIG GEOM)
```

EXERCISES

Evaluate the following:

1.   (LENGTH ' ( ))
2.   (LENGTH ' ((1 2 3 4 5)))
3.   (MEMBER 'VP ' (PRES VP SEC))
4.   (SUBST 'ASSISTANT 'SEC ' (STAFF (PRES VP SEC)))
5.   (REMOVE 'HAT ' (SCARF HAT GLOVES))

(SETF PIZZA ' ((MEAT (SAUSAGE HAM)) (VEGS (PEPPERS ONIONS))) CRUST SAUCE CHEESE)) Write expressions that will:

6. Determine the number of top-level items on the pizza.
7. Determine how many meat choices are on the pizza.
8. Reverse the order of top-level items.
9. Determine if cheese is a top-level item on the pizza.
10. Remove sausage from the meat items.
11. Replace ham with hamburger.
12. Reverse the vegetable choices.
13. Determine if peppers are a vegetable item.
14. Replace peppers with broccoli.

ANSWERS

1.   0
2.   1
3.   (VP SEC)
4.   (STAFF (PRES VP ASSISTANT))
5.   (SCARF GLOVES)
6.   (LENGTH PIZZA)
         returns 5
7.   (LENGTH (CAR (CDR (CAR PIZZA))))
         returns 2
8.   (REVERSE PIZZA)
         returns (CHEESE SAUCE CRUST (VEGS (PEPPERS ONIONS)) (MEAT (SAUSAGE HAM)))
9.   (MEMBER 'CHEESE PIZZA)
         returns (CHEESE)

10.   (REMOVE 'SAUSAGE (CAR (CDR (CAR PIZZA))))
          returns (HAM)

11.   (SUBST 'HAMBURGER 'HAM PIZZA)
          returns ((MEAT (SAUSAGE HAMBURGER)) (VEGS (PEPPERS ONIONS))
CRUST SAUCE CHEESE)

12.   (REVERSE (CAR (CDR (CAR (CDR PIZZA)))))
          returns (ONIONS PEPPERS)

13.   (MEMBER 'PEPPERS (CAR (CDR (CAR (CDR PIZZA)))))
          returns (PEPPERS ONIONS)

14.   (SUBST 'BROCCOLI 'PEPPERS PIZZA)
          returns ((MEAT (SAUSAGE HAM)) (VEGS (BROCCOLI ONIONS)
CRUST SAUCE CHEESE)

9

Predicate Functions

Predicate functions are those that return a value signaling either true or false. True is represented by the symbol T (or anything nonNIL), and false by the symbol NIL.

Function	Description
ATOM	is this an atom?
SYMBOLP	is this a symbol?
NUMBERP	is this a number?
LISTP	is this a list?
NULL	is this an empty list?
CONSP	is this a nonempty list?
MINUSP	is this number negative?
ZEROP	is this number 0?
PLUSP	is this number positive?
EVENP	is this number even?
ODDP	is this number odd?
<	test for less than
<=	test for less than or equal to
=	test for equal to
/=	test for not equal to
>	test for greater than
>=	test for greater than or equal to
EQ	are the expressions identical?
EQL	are the numbers or strings identical?
EQUAL	are the expressions equal?
NOT	is this false?
BOUNDP	has this symbol been assigned a value or defined?

ATOMIC PREDICATES

ATOM

format: (atom expr)

The ATOM function returns true if the expression is a symbolic atom, numeric atom, file, string, or object. Its argument should be quoted if a symbol to prevent evaluation of the symbol name.

Examples

```
> (atom '*)
T

> (atom 1)
T

> (atom "abc")
T

> (atom '(1 2 3))
NIL
```

SYMBOLP

format: (symbolp expr)

The SYMBOLP function returns true if the expression is a symbol. Its argument should be quoted to prevent evaluation of the symbol name.

Examples

```
> (symbolp '*)
T

> (symbolp 1)
NIL

> (symbolp "abc")
NIL

> (symbolp 'a)
T
```

NUMBERP

format: (numberp expr)

The NUMBERP function returns true if the expression is an integer or floating point number.

Examples

```
> (numberp 1)
T

> (numberp (* 8 7))
T

> (numberp 2.56)
T

> (numberp '*)
NIL

> (numberp '(* 8 7))
NIL
```

LIST PREDICATES

LISTP

format: (listp expr)

The LISTP function determines if the expression is a valid list.

Examples

```
> (listp '(a b c))
T

> (listp 1)
NIL

> (listp '*)
NIL

> (listp (* 8 7))
NIL
```

```
> (listp '(* 8 7))
T

> (listp '())
T

> (listp NIL)              ;NIL is equivalent to (), the null list
T

> (setf a '(1 2 3))
(1 2 3)

> (listp a)
T
```

NULL

format: (null expr)

The function NULL returns true if the expression is an empty list.

Examples

```
> (setf letter '(a))
(A)

> (null letter)
NIL

> (cdr letter)
NIL

> (null (cdr letter))      ; (null NIL) is True
T
```

CONSP

format: (consp expr)

The CONSP function returns true if the list expression contains any elements, that is, it is not the null list.

Examples

```
> (consp letter)
T
```

```
> (consp (cdr letter))
NIL
```

INTEGER PREDICATES

PLUSP, MINUSP, ZEROP, EVENP, ODDP

```
                              format: (plusp expr)
```

The PLUSP, MINUSP, ZEROP, EVENP, ODDP functions determine if the integer argument is positive, negative, zero, odd, or even.

Examples

```
> (setf a 1 b -2)
-2

> (plusp a)
T

> (plusp b)
NIL

> (minusp a)
NIL

> (minusp b)
T

> (evenp a)
NIL

> (evenp b)
T

> (oddp a)
T

> (oddp b)
NIL

> (zerop (+ a b 1))
T
```

RELATIONAL PREDICATES

<, <=, =, /=, >, >=

format: (< expr1 expr2)

The relational predicates can be used to compare integers or strings. The value of a character is its numeric ASCII value. A character with a lower ASCII value will be less than a character whose ASCII value is greater. When comparing string values, the relational predicates check the ASCII values of each character on the strings from left to right. A value is returned when a nonmatching character is found or when the end of the first string is reached.

Examples

```
> (< 1 2)              ;1 is less than 2
T

> (> 1 2)              ;1 is not greater than 2
NIL

> (= "abc" "abc")      ;the strings are equal
T

> (char "a" 0)         ;return ASCII value
97

> (char "A" 0)         ;return ASCII value
65

> (= "abc" "ABC")      ;these strings are not equal
NIL

> (< "a" "b")
T

> (< "b" "a")
NIL

> (char "c" 0)         ;return ASCII value
99

> (char "d" 0)         ;return ASCII value
100

> (< "abc" "abd")      ;can be used for alphabetic comparisons
T
```

EQUALITY PREDICATES

There are several predicate functions available for testing equality of the various data types in LISP. These functions can determine equality depending upon either the internal representation of the item or the printed representation. For purposes of discussion in this section, the term *object* refers to the internal representation of an item.

EQ

```
format:  (eq elt1 elt2)
```

The EQ function returns true only if elt1 and elt2 are the same object. In LISP, you are allowed to make copies of elements. These copies appear identical, but LISP identifies them as distinct objects. Therefore, lists and strings that have the same elements and whose printed representations appear identical are not necessarily equal according to the evaluation of this function. The examples below demonstrate this function.

Examples

1. Integers

```
>  (eq 1 1)
NIL

>  (setf a 2)
2

>  (eq a 2)
NIL

>  (eq a a)
T
```

2. Lists

```
>  (setf num1 '(1 2 3))
(1 2 3)

>  (setf num2 '(1 2 3))
(1 2 3)

>  (eq num1 num2)              ;different lists
NIL

>  (setf num3 num1)
(1 2 3)

>  (eq num3 num1)              ;same list
T
```

3. Strings

```
> (setf s "aaa")
"aaa"

> (eq s "aaa")
NIL

> (setf s1 "aaa")
"aaa"

> (setf s2 s1)
"aaa"

> (eq s s1)                    ;different strings
NIL

> (eq s2 s1)                   ;same strings
T
```

EQL

```
format:  (eql elt1 elt2)
```

The EQL function returns true if elt1 and elt2 are the same object (as evaluated for the function EQ above). In addition, the function EQL further compares the values of numbers or strings. If elt1 and elt2 are the same number, the function returns true. If elt1 and elt2 are strings and have the same printed representation, true will be returned.

Examples

1. Integers

```
> (eql 1 1)
T

> (setf a 2)
2

> (eql a 2)
T

> (eql a a)
T
```

2. Lists

```
> (setf num1 '(1 2 3))
(1 2 3)
```

```
> (setf num2 '(1 2 3))
(1 2 3)

> (eql num1 num2)
NIL

> (setf num3 num1)
(1 2 3)

> (eql num3 num1)
T
```

3. Strings

```
> (setf s "aaa")
"aaa"

> (eql s "aaa")
T

> (setf s1 "aaa")
"aaa"

> (setf s2 s1)
"aaa"

> (eql s s1)
T

> (eql s2 s1)
T
```

EQUAL

```
format:  (equal elt1 elt2)
```

The EQUAL function returns true if elt1 and elt2 have the same printed representations. Characters, numbers, strings, and lists can be compared using this function. Lists and strings need not be the same objects; copies can be compared for equality.

Examples

1. Integers

```
> (equal 1 1)
T

> (setf a 2)
2
```

```
> (equal a 2)
T

> (equal a a)
T
```

2. Lists

```
> (setf num1 '(1 2 3))
(1 2 3)

> (setf num2 '(1 2 3))
(1 2 3)

> (equal num1 num2)
T

> (setf num3 num1)
(1 2 3)

> (equal num3 num1)
T
```

3. Strings

```
> (setf s "aaa")
"aaa"
> (equal s "aaa")
T

> (setf s1 "aaa")
"aaa"

> (setf s2 s1)
"aaa"

> (equal s s1)
T
> (equal s2 s1)
T
```

Remember, the EQUAL function is used to verify that the printed representations of items are the same. EQ verifies that the internal representations point to the same object. EQL is similar to EQ, except that it further compares the printed representations of numbers and strings. Which equality test do you use when implementing a LISP program? It depends upon whether you are comparing only printed representations or whether you need to know the internal representation of an item. The computational cost of using the EQUAL function can be greater because the interpreter must further check each corresponding element of the list.

MISCELLANEOUS PREDICATES

NOT

format: (not expr)

The NOT function returns true if the expression evaluates to false.

Examples

```
> (not nil)
T

> (not '())
T

> (not T)
NIL

> (not (null letter))   ; remember, letter =   '(a)
T

> letter
(a)

> (not (consp letter))
NIL

> (not (listp '(a b c)))
NIL
```

BOUNDP

format: (boundp expr)

The BOUNDP function determines if a symbol has been assigned a value.

Examples

```
> (boundp '*)         ;the symbol "*" is bound to the statements
                      ;defining the multiplication function
T

> (boundp 'sym)
NIL
```

```
> (setf sym 1)        ;assign value
1

> (boundp 'sym)       ;sym is now bound
T
```

EXERCISES

1. Define a predicate function TEMP-SAME that takes two arguments, a Fahrenheit and a Centigrade temperature. The function will return the symbol T if they are equivalent temperatures and NIL if not. The formula for Fahrenheit to Centigrade conversion is

$$cent = (fahr - 32) * 5/9$$

2. Write a predicate procedure COMPARE that returns the atom T if the first element on a list is less than the last element.
3. Write a predicate function that takes two arguments, an element and a list. The function EMPTY returns the atom T if the list is null when the element is removed. NIL is returned if the list is not null when the element is removed.
4. Write a predicate function LONGER-LIST that takes two lists as arguments and returns the atom T if the first list is longer than the second.
5. Write the predicate function SUMCOMPARE that takes four numbers as arguments and returns the atom T if the sum of the first two arguments equals the sum of the last two.

ANSWERS

```
1. (defun TEMP-SAME (fahr cent)
        (= cent (truncate (* (- fahr 32.0) (/ 5.0 9.0))))))
2. (defun COMPARE (L) (< (car L) (car (last L))))
3. (defun EMPTY (L item)
        (null (remove item L)))
4. (defun LONGER-LIST (L M)
        (> (length L) (length M)))
5. (defun SUMCOMPARE (w x y z)
        (= (+ w x) (+ y z)))
```

10

Conditional Forms

Procedure	Description
IF	execute expressions conditionally
COND	evaluate conditionally
AND	the logical AND of a list of expressions
OR	the logical OR of a list of expressions

EVALUATING CONDITIONALLY

IF

```
format: (if condition result)
```

The procedure IF is used when there is only one condition to evaluate. If the condition is true, the result will be evaluated.

Examples

1. If data type is a list, return length.

```
> (defun LIST-LENGTH (L)
1> (if (listp L) (length L)))        ;if list, return the length
LIST-LENGTH
```

```
> (LIST-LENGTH '(1 2 3 4))
4

> (LIST-LENGTH '★)
NIL
```

2. If data type is numeric, return absolute value.

```
> (defun MAKE-POSITIVE (num)
1> (if (numberp num) (abs num)))       ;if numeric, return absolute value
MAKE-POSITIVE

> (MAKE-POSITIVE (★ 2 10))
20

> (MAKE-POSITIVE -10)
10

> (MAKE-POSITIVE '(-10))
NIL
```

IF (With Optional Result)

```
format: (if condition result optional-result)
```

Another format of the IF conditional specifies an optional result expression. If the condition is false, the result is not evaluated, but defaults to the optional-result expression. This is like an if-then-else in other programming languages.

Example

1. Redefine LIST-LENGTH with optional result field.

```
> (defun LIST-LENGTH (L)
1> (if (listp L) (length L) 'NOT-A-LIST))
LIST-LENGTH

> (LIST-LENGTH '(1 2 3 4))
4

> (LIST-LENGTH '*)
NOT-A-LIST
```

COND

The special form COND allows you to select a clause to evaluate from a list of clauses. It is similar to the if-then-else statements or "case" statements in other programming languages. In the "C" programming language, you may be familiar with the "switch" statement, and in PL1, the ''select'' statement. Each argument to COND is a list containing a condition and its corresponding result. The conditions that COND evaluates are most often predicate functions that evaluate to true or false. This special form has the following format:

```
(cond ( <condition-1> <result-1> . . . )
      ( <condition-2> <result-2> . . . )
      . . .
      ( <condition-n> <result-n> . . . )
      ( T <default-result> . . . ))
```

The arguments are evaluated left to right as follows:

```
If the value of condition-1 is not NIL,
   then the value of COND is the value of the last result-1
         expression; else
.
.
.
.
.
If the value of condition-n is not NIL,
   then the value of COND is the value of the last result-n
         expression; else
Default to the special symbol T, return default-result.
```

If condition-1 evaluates to true (T), the sequence of result-1 statements is evaluated, its value returned and evaluation stops here. If condition-1 is false (NIL), the next condition is evaluated. Evaluation stops when a condition evaluates true, i.e., anything nonNIL. If all the conditions are false, it will default to the last statement, since the symbol T always evaluates to true. It is good programming practice to default to T, since this will make the programs readable and the default obvious. Note that the result is never evaluated if the corresponding condition is false.

Examples

1. Determine if a specified symbol is a member of a list.

```
> (setf fruit '(peach plum pear pineapple))
(PEACH PLUM PEAR PINEAPPLE)

> (cond ((member 'plum fruit))        ; condition-1 and result-1
⊥>       (T 'NO-PLUMS))                ; default
(PLUM PEAR PINEAPPLE)
```

In this example, the condition-1 statement does double duty, since it is also the result-1 statement. The MEMBER predicate returns a list containing the element, which is interpreted as true. This list also becomes the result of evaluating the COND.

2. Using DEFUN, determine if a number is positive, negative, or zero.

```
> (defun NUMBER-TYPE (num)
1> (cond ((zerop num) 'zero)
2>        ((plusp num) 'positive)
2>        (T           'negative)))        ;default
NUMBER-TYPE

> (NUMBER-TYPE 18)
POSITIVE

> (NUMBER-TYPE 0)
ZERO

> (NUMBER-TYPE -80)
NEGATIVE
```

3. Determine length of a list.

```
> (defun LIST-LENGTH (L)
1> (cond (listp L) (length L))        ;if list, return the length
2>        (T     'NOT-A-LIST)))        ;otherwise return message
LIST-LENGTH

> (LIST-LENGTH '(1 2 3))
3

> (LIST-LENGTH '*)
NOT-A-LIST
```

4. Convert characters to numbers.

```
> (defun CHAR-TO-NUM (ch)
1>    (cond ((= ch "0")  0)        ;case 0
2>          ((= ch "1")  1)        ;case 1
2>          ((= ch "2")  2)        ;case 2
2>          ((= ch "3")  3)        ;case 3
2>          ((= ch "4")  4)        ;case 4
2>          ((= ch "5")  5)        ;case 5
2>          ((= ch "6")  6)        ;case 6
2>          ((= ch "7")  7)        ;case 7
2>          ((= ch "8")  8)        ;case 8
2>          ((= ch "9")  9)        ;case 9
2>          (T NIL)))        ;default case, return NIL
CHAR-TO-NUM

> (CHAR-TO-NUM "0")
0
```

```
>  (CHAR-TO-NUM  "9")
9

>  (CHAR-TO-NUM  "7")
7

>  (CHAR-TO-NUM  "A")
NIL
```

This lengthy COND statement can be simplified using the special form AND described below.

· LOGICAL CONNECTIVES

The logical connectives AND and OR enable you to test multiple conditions. They evaluate their arguments from left to right and return either true T or NIL. These functions can take an indefinite number of arguments. .

AND

```
format:  (and statement-1 . . . statement-n)
```

The special form AND evaluates its arguments in sequence from left to right. It stops its evaluation when it encounters an argument that evaluates to NIL or when the end of the list of arguments is reached. The value of AND is true if all its arguments are nonNIL. The value of AND is NIL if any argument is NIL. Remaining arguments on the list are not evaluated once a NIL value is encountered.

Examples

1. Testing for values zero through nine can be done in one statement:

```
(and  (>= ch "0")  (<= ch "9"))
```

Used with the IF statement, the complex COND statement above that converts ASCII characters to integer values can be simplified as follows:

```
>  (defun CHAR-TO-NUM  (ch)
1>  (if  (and  (>= ch "0")  (<= ch "9"))  (- (char ch 0) (char "0"  0))
'NOT-NUMERIC))
CHAR-TO-NUM

>  (CHAR-TO-NUM  "2")
2

>  (CHAR-TO-NUM  "Z")
NOT-NUMERIC
```

2. Changing lower-case characters to upper-case characters is done as follows:

```
> (defun LOWER-TO-UPPER (ch)
1> (if (and (>= ch "a") (<= ch "z")) (string (- (char ch 0)   32)))))
LOWER-TO-UPPER

> (LOWER-TO-UPPER "f")
"F"

> (LOWER-TO-UPPER "q")
"Q"

> (LOWER-TO-UPPER "3")
NIL
```

OR

```
                           format: (or statement-1 . . . statement-n)
```

  The special form OR evaluates its arguments in sequence from left to right. It stops its evaluation when it encounters an argument that evaluates to nonNIL or when the end of the list of arguments is reached. The value of OR is true if any of its arguments are nonNIL. Remaining arguments on the list are not evaluated once a nonNIL value is encountered. The value of OR is NIL if all arguments are NIL.

Examples

1. Determine if a character is not lower-case alphabetic.

```
> (defun LOWER-CASE (ch)
1> (if (or (< ch "a") (> ch "z")) 'NOT-LOWER 'LOWER))
LOWER-CASE

> (LOWER-CASE "x")
LOWER

> (LOWER-CASE "A")
NOT-LOWER
```

2. The following predicate procedure (combining AND and OR) determines if a year is a leap year. Remember, a century year is not a leap year unless it is divisible by 400.

```
> (defun LEAP (year)
1> (or (= 0 (rem year 400))            ;century year
2>       (and (/= 0 (rem year 100))    ;not a century year
3>             (= 0 (rem year 4)))))   ;divisible by 4
LEAP
```

> **(LEAP 1986)**
NIL

> **(LEAP 1988)**
T

> **(LEAP 1900)**
NIL

> **(LEAP 2000)**
T

EXERCISES

1. Write the predicate function ALPHABETIC that returns true if a character argument is either an upper-case or lower-case character.
2. Write the procedure POSTAGE that takes the cost of an item and returns the postage charge according to the following table:

Item Cost	Postage Charge
under $25.00	$3.50
$25.01 to $50.00	$4.25
$50.01 to $75.00	$5.00
$75.01 to $100.00	$5.75
over $100.00	$6.50

3. Write the predicate function X-MEMBER that returns T if an item is a top-level element of a list; otherwise it returns NIL. Verify that the first argument passed is a list.
4. Write the predicate function MEMBER-BOTH that takes two items and a list as arguments. Determine if both items are members of the list.
5. Write the predicate function MEMBER-EITHER that takes one item and two lists as arguments. Determine if the item is a member of either list.

ANSWERS

1. (defun ALPHABETIC (ch)
     (if (or (and (>= ch "A") (<= ch "Z"))
             (and (>= ch "a") (<= ch "z"))) t))

2. (defun POSTAGE (item)
   (cond ((<= item 25.00) 3.50)
         ((<= item 50.00) 4.25)
         ((<= item 75.00) 5.00)
         ((<= item 100.00) 5.75)
         (T 6.25)))

3. (defun X-MEMBER (L thing)
   (if (and (listp L) (member thing L)) T))

4. (defun MEMBER-BOTH (L this that)
     (if (and (member this L) (member that L)) T))

5. (defun MEMBER-EITHER (L M this)
     (if (or (member this L) (member this M)) T))

11

Looping, Iteration, and Sequencing Procedures

Procedure	Description
DOTIMES	iterate *n* times
DOLIST	iterate for each element of a list
DO	iterate conditionally
DO*	iterate conditionally, initialize, and update values sequentially

One of the simplest ways to repetitively compute the numeric value of one or more variables is to use a DO loop construct. This is very similar to the DO procedures in many other programming languages, such as BASIC or FORTRAN. The DOTIMES and DOLIST procedures are specific procedures that are applied to sequences of integers and lists, respectively. The following extremely simple examples illustrate the various DO constructs.

LOOPING PROCEDURES

DOTIMES

```
format: (dotimes (symbol value) <body>)
```

The procedure DOTIMES allows you to iterate a specified number of times through a loop. The expression after the function name initializes (binds) a symbol to a value. The function iterates from 0 to value-1 and returns NIL. (Note: The function PRINT in these examples sends a character representation of some value to standard output, the screen.)

Example

```
> (dotimes (a 4)        ;values 0 through 3 are printed on s eparate lines
1>      (print a))      ;NIL is returned
0
1
2
3
NIL
```

DOTIMES (With Optional Result)

```
format: (dotimes (symbol value optional-result) <body>)
```

An optional expression can follow that specifies the result to return when the loop has been completed. If there is no result expression, the loop returns NIL, as in the example above.

Example

```
> (dotimes (a 3 'ALL-DONE)
1>      (print a))
0
1
2
ALL-DONE
```

The next example converts a string of characters from lower-case to upper-case. Only alphabetic characters are changed.

Examples

```
> (defun LOWER-TO-UPPER (lower &aux upper ch)
1> (setf upper " ")
1> (dotimes (a (length lower))
2>      (setf ch (substr lower (+ a 1) 1))
2>      (if (and (>= ch "a") (<= ch "z"))
3>          (setf upper (strcat upper (string (- (char ch 0) 32))))
3>          (setf upper (strcat upper ch))))
1> (print upper))
LOWER-TO-UPPER

> (LOWER-TO-UPPER "abcx")
"ABCX"
```

```
>  (LOWER-TO-UPPER "John Doe")
"JOHN DOE"

>  (LOWER-TO-UPPER "94% Free?")
"94% FREE?"
```

DOLIST

```
format:  (dolist (symbol list optional-result) <body>)
```

The procedure DOLIST allows you to iterate through a list of elements. The expression after the function name initializes (binds) a symbol to each element on the specified list. The function iterates down the list for each element on the list. As in the DOTIMES example, an optional expression can follow that specifies the result to return when the loop has been completed. If there is no result expression, the loop returns NIL.

Examples

```
>  (setf zoo-list '("LIONS" "TIGERS" "BEARS"))
("LIONS" "TIGERS" "BEARS")
>  (dolist (a zoo-list zoo-list)
1>     (print a))
"LIONS"
"TIGERS"
"BEARS"
("LIONS" "TIGERS" "BEARS")
```

The next example takes a list of integers as its argument and returns the sum of the integers on the list.

```
>  (defun ADD-LIST (num-list &aux sum)
1>     (setf sum 0)
1>     (dolist (x num-list sum)
2>          (setf sum (+ sum x))
2>     ))
ADD-LIST

>  (ADD-LIST '(1 2 3))
6

>  (ADD-LIST '(10 -100 90))
0

>  (ADD-LIST '(20 30 40 -1))
89
```

DO

```
format:  (do ((symbol-1 value-1) . . . (symbol-n value-n))
             (test-expr optional-result)
             <body>)
```

In the examples above, the iterations are done for a specified number of times, or through a specified list of elements. When we want to iterate an unknown number of times until a certain condition is true, we must use the DO procedure. As previously, the expression after the function name initializes (binds) symbols to initial values. (Note that the initialization expressions are evaluated for each symbol before the values are assigned to the symbols. This is discussed in detail later.) The function terminates when the test expression evaluates true.

As in the DOTIMES and DOLIST procedures, an optional expression can follow the test expression that specifies the result to return when the loop has been completed. If there is no result expression, the loop returns NIL.

This example prompts you for integer values. Enter NIL when you are finished. (The function READ allows the procedure to obtain integer values from you at the terminal.) The procedure then returns the average of the list of numbers.

Example

```
> (defun AVERAGE ()
1>     (do ((value 0)(total 0)(count 0))
2>         ((eq value nil) (/ total (1- count)))
2>     (setf total (+ total value))
2>     (setf count (1+ count))
2>     (print "Enter integer value, NIL to terminate")
2>     (setf value (read))
2>     ))
AVERAGE

> (AVERAGE)
"Enter integer value, NIL to terminate"

> 10
"Enter integer value, NIL to terminate"

> 20
"Enter integer value, NIL to terminate"

> 30
"Enter integer value, NIL to terminate"

> 40
"Enter integer value, NIL to terminate"

> NIL
25
```

DO (With Optional Step Increment)

```
format (do ((symbol-1 value-1 optional-step) . . .
            (symbol-n value-n optional-step))
           (test-expr optional-result)
           <body>)
```

An optional step expression can be specified to allow automatic incrementing. This eliminates the need for an incrementing expression within the loop. In the integer-averaging example, the symbol count can be incremented automatically, as follows:

Example

```
> (defun AVERAGE2 ()
1>     (do ((value 0)(total 0)(count 0 (1+ count)))
2>         ((eq value nil)
3>                       (list 'AVERAGE (/ total (1- count)))))
2>     (setf total (+ total value))
2>     (print "Enter integer value, NIL to terminate")
2>     (setf value (read))
2>     ))
AVERAGE2


> (AVERAGE2)
"Enter integer value, NIL to terminate"

> 10
"Enter integer value, NIL to terminate"

> 20
"Enter integer value, NIL to terminate"

> 30
"Enter integer value, NIL to terminate"

> 40
"Enter integer value, NIL to terminate"

> NIL
(AVERAGE 25)
```

INITIALIZATIONS

As noted above, the initialization expressions are evaluated for each symbol before the values are assigned to the symbols. In the example above, the two symbols ''value'' and ''total'' were independent of each other, and both were initialized to the value 0.

In the next example, the value of the symbol ''total'' depends upon the value of the symbol *''value.''* The value for the symbol ''value'' is not assigned until all the initializations are completed. Since the value of the symbol ''total'' depends on the symbol ''value,'' it will be unbound when the function is evaluated. An error will be generated.

Example

```
> (defun ERR-AVERAGE ()
1>     (do ((value 0)(total value)(count 0 (1+ count)))
2>         ((eq value nil)
3>                         (list 'AVERAGE (/ total (1- count))))
2>     (setf total (+ total value))
2>     (print "Enter integer value, NIL to terminate")
2>     (setf value (read))
2>     ))
ERR-AVERAGE

> (ERR-AVERAGE)
error - unbound variable - VALUE
if continued: try evaluating symbol again

1: > (clean-up)
[abort to previous level]
>
```

DO*

```
format: (do* ((symbol-1 value-1 optional-step) . . .
              (symbol-n value-n optional-step))
             (test-expr optional-result)
             <body>)
```

The function DO* allows the symbols to be bound to initialization expressions in order. This function eliminates the error in the example above, where the values of the initialization for the symbol ''total'' depend upon the initialization of the symbol ''value.''

```
> (defun AVERAGE* ()
1>     (do* ((value 0)(total value)(count 0 (1+ count)))
2>         ((eq value NIL)
3>                         (list 'AVERAGE (/ total (1- count))))
2>     (setf total (+ total value))
2>     (print "Enter integer value, NIL to terminate")
2>     (setf value (read))
2>     ))
AVERAGE*
```

```
>  (AVERAGE*)
"Enter integer value, NIL to terminate"

>  10
"Enter integer value, NIL to terminate"

>  20
"Enter integer value, NIL to terminate"

>  30
"Enter integer value, NIL to terminate"

>  NIL
(AVERAGE 20)
```

ITERATIONS ON LISTS

Procedure	Description
MAPCAR	apply function to successive CARS
MAPLIST	apply function to successive CDRS

LISP provides several functions that allow you to apply procedures to each element on a list. This is known as *mapping*. The result is a list containing the values of the procedure application for each respective element of the list.

MAPCAR

```
                format: (mapcar procedure list1 . . . listn)
```

The MAPCAR function allows you to apply a procedure to each element on a list. The arguments to this function must be a procedure name followed by lists of elements. There must be a list for each argument that the function expects. (For example, the function ABS expects one argument; therefore, MAPCAR expects one list of elements. The function + expects at least two arguments; MAPCAR must be given at least two lists when this function is used.) MAPCAR returns a list of the evaluations of each element on the list by the specified procedure.

```
>  (mapcar 'zerop '(0 1 2 0 3 4 5))     ;determine which elements are zero
(T NIL NIL T NIL NIL NIL)

>  (mapcar 'abs '(0 1 2 0 -1 -2))       ;return list of absolute values
(0 1 2 0 1 2)

>  (mapcar '+ '(0 1 2) '(2 3 4))        ;return list of addition results
(2 4 6)
```

MAPLIST

format: (maplist procedure list1 . . . listn)

The MAPLIST function allows you to apply a procedure to each successive CDR of a list. The arguments to this function must be a procedure name followed by lists of elements. There must be a list for each argument that the function expects. The function returns a list of the evaluations of each successive CDR of the list by the specified procedure. The following example reverses successive CDRS:

```
> (maplist 'reverse '(I WAS HERE))
((HERE WAS I) (HERE WAS) (HERE))
```

The next example appends successive CDRS:

```
> (maplist 'append '(PENNIES FROM HEAVEN) '(FELL MY WAY))
((PENNIES FROM HEAVEN FELL MY WAY)
(FROM HEAVEN MY WAY)
(HEAVEN WAY)
```

SEQUENCING

Procedure	Description
PROG1	Return value of first form evaluated in a sequence of forms
PROG2	Return value of second form evaluated in a sequence of forms
PROGN	Return value of last form evaluated in a sequence of forms

PROG1

format: (prog1 statement-1 . . . statement-n)

PROG2

format: (prog2 statement-1 . . . statement-n)

PROGN

format: (progn statement-1 . . . statement-n)

The procedures listed above are used to group together sequences of statements. The statements are executed in order and evaluated for their side effects. The only difference is the value that is returned. PROG1 returns the value of the first statement in the series; PROG2 returns the value of the second statement in the series; PROGN returns the value of the last statement.

Examples

1. PROG1
```
> (prog1 (setf apple (list 'red 'round))
>        (setf color (car apple))
>        (setf shape (cadr apple))))
```

(RED ROUND)

2. PROG2
```
> (prog2 (setf apple (list 'red 'round))
>        (setf color (car apple))
>        (setf shape (cadr apple))))
```

RED

3. PROGN
```
> (progn (setf apple (list 'red 'round))
>        (setf color (car apple))
>        (setf shape (cadr apple))))
```

ROUND

EXERCISES

1. Using the predicate function LEAP defined in the previous chapter, write the procedure DAY-OF-YEAR that takes three arguments—the month, day, and year—and returns the numeric day of the year. For example:

   (DAY-OF-YEAR 1 1 1986) returns 1
   (DAY-OF-YEAR 2 1 1986) returns 32
   (DAY-OF-YEAR 3 1 1986) returns 60
   (DAY-OF-YEAR 1 1 1988) returns 1
   (DAY-OF-YEAR 2 1 1988) returns 32
   (DAY-OF-YEAR 3 1 1988) returns 61

2. Using a DO construct, define the procedure FAHR-TO-CENT that takes as its argument a list of Fahrenheit temperatures and returns the corresponding list of Centigrade temperatures. (Hint: Write the function F-TO-C that converts Fahrenheit to Centigrade using the formula: C = (F − 32) * 5/9. Call F-TO-C from FAHR-TO-CENT.)

   (FAHR-TO-CENT '(100 32 0 −40)) returns (37 0 −17 −40)

3. Redefine FAHR-TO-CENT using MAPCAR instead of the DO construct.
4. Define the function X-MAX that returns the maximum value on a list of positive numbers. Do not use the built-in function MAX; rather use a DO construct to compare the numbers on the list.

>   (X-MAX '(1 2 3)) returns 3
>   (X-MAX '(20 40 30 10)) returns 40
>   (X-MAX '(100 999 876 2)) returns 999

5. The number of students attending a certain college is projected to increase at a rate of 5 percent each year. If the college currently has 1000 students, what will be the percentage increase in the student population after x years? Write the procedure POPULATION that takes as its argument the number of years and returns the projected number of students.
6. Define the procedure LEAP? that takes as its argument a list of years. Use the function MAPCAR and the function LEAP to return the list showing which years are leap years (T) or NIL if not.

>   (LEAP? '(1986 1988 1990 1992 1996))
>   (NIL T NIL T T)

ANSWERS

```
1. (defun DAY-OF-YEAR (month day year &aux day-array)
   (setf day-array '(31 28 31 30 31 30 31 31 30 31 30 31))
   (if (and (> month 2) (LEAP year))
        (setf day (1+ day)))
   (dotimes (count (1- month) day)
        (setf day (+ day (nth count day-array)))))))

   (defun LEAP (year)
     (or (= 0 (rem year 400))              ;century year
         (and (/= 0 (rem year 100))        ;not a century year
              (= 0 (rem year 4)))))        ;divisible by 4?
2. (defun FAHR-TO-CENT (fahr-list &aux cent-list)
     (setf cent-list '())
     (dolist (temp fahr-list cent-list)
       (setf cent-list (append cent-list (list (F-TO-C temp))))))

   (defun F-TO-C (fahr)
     (truncate (* (- fahr 32.0) (/ 5.0 9.0))))
3. (defun FAHR-TO-CENT (fahr-list)
     (mapcar 'F-TO-C fahr-list))
```

4. (defun X-MAX (L &aux max-value)
   (setf max-value 0)
   (dolist (num L max-value)
      (if (> num max-value)(setf max-value num))))

5. (defun POPULATION (year &aux pop)
   (do ((pop 1000))
      ((<= year 0) (truncate pop))
   (setf pop (* 1.05 pop))
   (setf year (1- year))))

6. (defun LEAP? (year-list)
   (mapcar 'LEAP year-list))

12

A Discussion About Bindings

An in-depth discussion of bindings can be found in Winston and Horn's *LISP, Second Edition.** The discussion that follows here introduces you to the concept.

LISP is a "call-by-value" programming language. This means that the value of a symbol is passed as the argument to a function and not the symbol itself. The value of the symbol that is passed is bound, or assigned, to the parameter name in the called function.

A symbol is bound if it has a value assigned to it. This can be done by initializing a symbol with the procedures SETQ or SETF. You can also temporarily bind the value of a symbol to a parameter by calling a function with the symbol name as an argument, by binding it in one of the DO loops, or by using the function LET. The collection of bindings within a procedure or a loop is called an *environment*.

BINDING SYMBOLS AND FUNCTIONS

The function BOUNDP can be used to determine if a symbol has been bound. Its argument must be a quoted symbol, or an error is generated. Try the following examples:

*Patrick Henry Winston and Berthold Klaus Paul Horn, *LISP, Second Edition*, (Reading, Mass.: Addison-Wesley Publishing Co., 1984).

Examples

1.

```
> (boundp 'sym)      ;test if sym is bo und to a value
NIL

> (setf sym 1)       ;bind sym to a value using SETF
1

> (boundp 'sym)      ;sym is now bound
T

> sym                ;typing symbol name gives its value
1
```

2.

```
> (boundp 'x)                  ;x is not  bound
NIL

> (defun SQUARE (x) (* x x))   ;DEFUN binds   the symbol SQUARE
                               ;to the instructions necessary
                               ;to square a number

SQUARE

> (boundp 'SQUARE)             ;SQUARE is now bound
T

> (boundp 'x)                  ;x is unbound  outside of the
                               ;function SQUARE

NIL

> SQUARE                       ;typing function name
                               ;shows the   internal
                               ;code generated  by XLISP

((LAMBDA (X)  (* X X)))
```

3. In this example, you notice that the symbol x is bound to the value 2. When the function SQUARE is called, the value of x is bound temporarily to the parameter passed to the function SQUARE. The value of the symbol x is reinitialized to its original value outside of the function environment.

```
> (setf x 2)      ;assign a value to x
2

> (SQUARE 3)      ;call the function SQUARE
                  ;inside the function, x is temporarily
                  ;bound to the value 3
9

> x               ;exiting the function restores original value
2
```

BINDING WITHIN A DO ENVIRONMENT

This example demonstrates why you should be careful when initializing parameters within a DO environment. The symbol total is initialized to the value of the symbol "value" outside of the DO environment. The value of "total" is incorrectly initialized to 100, without generating an error message for you. The result of executing the function returns the average of the numbers you input and incorrectly adds 100 to the total before computing the average. The function DO* would generate the correct initializations.

```
> (setf value 100)
100


> (defun ERR-AVERAGE ()
1>     (do ((value 0)(total value)(count 0 (1+ count)))
2>          ((eq value NIL)(print
4>                          (list "AVERAGE:" (/ total (1- count)))))
2>     (setf total (+ total value))
2>     (print "Enter integer value, NIL to terminate")
2>     (setf value (read))
2>     ))
ERR-AVERAGE


> (ERR-AVERAGE)
"Enter integer value, NIL to terminate"


> 10
"Enter integer value, NIL to terminate"


> 20
"Enter integer value, NIL to terminate"


> NIL
("AVERAGE: " 65)
("AVERAGE: " 65)


> value
100
```

USING LET TO BIND AND EVALUATE

LET

```
format: (let ((symbol-1 init-expr1) (. . .)
              (symbol-n init-exprn))
         <body>)
```

The function LET allows you to assign values to parameters and evaluate expressions containing these parameters. Its argument is a list consisting of symbol name and initialization pairs, followed by expressions to evaluate. This function creates an environment for the parameters initialized here. Just as in the DO procedure, the initializations are evaluated before the parameters are assigned their new values; that is, they are assigned their values in parallel.

LET*

```
format:  (let* ((symbol-1 init-expr1) (. . .)
                (symbol-n init-exprn))
         <body>)
```

The procedure LET* allows you to assign values to your parameters as they are encountered (sequentially), similar to the procedure DO*.

Examples

1. > (setf a 5)
  5

  > (let ((a 1))   ;bind *a* to value 1
  1>   (* a 2))   ;evaluate expression
  2

  > a   ;*a* is restored to original value
  5

2. > (let ((a 1) (b 2))   ;initialize *a* and *b* independently
  1>   (* a b))
  2

  > a   ;*a* is restored to original value
  5

  > (boundp 'b)   ;*b* is unbound outside of the procedure
  NIL

3. This example demonstrates the order of initializations. An error is generated if the symbol *a* is unbound outside of the let environment, similar to the error generated in the procedure ERR-AVERAGE in the previous chapter.

```
> a
5

> (let ((a 2)              ;evaluate initialization
2>         (b a))           ;evaluate initialization, b depends on a
                            ;a is now set to 2 ;b is set to 5
1>       (* a b))           ;evaluate expression
10
```

4. The procedure LET* produces a different result. The value of the symbol *b* depends upon the value of the symbol *a* within the LET* environment.

```
> a
5

> (let* ((a 2)             ;initialize a to 2
2>         (b a))           ;initialize b to 2, b depends on a
1>       (* a b))           ;evaluate expression
4

> a                        ;value of a is restored
5
```

13

Association and Property Lists

In LISP, as in most other programming languages, we often want to group facts about an item of data together. The best way to do this is to create a list of attributes associated with the item. For example, a personnel database may need to group together the job description, blood type, personality type, and location of all the employees in a company. This information would constitute a "record" describing an employee.

In PASCAL, we can initialize a record in a program as follows:

```
record
      job : array [1..24] of Char;
      has-blood : (A, B, AB, 0);
      personality : array [1..30] of Char;
      is-located : array [1..30] of Char;
   end
```

If the variable employee-1 had been initialized to be a record of the type described, we could access the fields by referencing employee-1.job, employee-1.has-blood, and so forth. This is fine if the database has been well defined and contains all the information that will ever be needed. If, however, we need to add information to each employee's record, such as date-of-hire, we would have to modify this record and recompile the program.

We do not have this problem in LISP. We have ways of creating an open-ended database using association lists or property lists. It is very easy to add attributes to these lists without disturbing the structure of the program. These procedures demonstrate the power of the LISP programming language.

ASSOCIATION LISTS

The LISP data structure that allows us to create a database that the LISP functions will understand is called an *association list*. The following is an example of creating such a list:

```
> (setf employee-1 '((job president)
2>                    (has-blood A)
2>                    (personality optimist)
2>                    (is-located ivory-tower)))

((JOB PRESIDENT) (HAS-BLOOD A) (PERSONALITY OPTIMIST)
    (IS-LOCATED IVORY-TOWER))
```

An association list is a list containing sublists, each of which contains a key symbol and datum. The key is the first element on each of the sublists. In the example above, the symbols job, has-blood, personality, and is-located are the key items. The datum associated with each key is the second element on each sublist. (The term *association list* is often abbreviated as *a-list*.)

FIND AN EXPRESSION IN AN A-LIST

ASSOC

```
                format: (assoc key a-list)
```

ASSOC will search the a-list and return the entire sublist containing the key. If no match exists, NIL is returned.

```
> (assoc 'has-blood employee-1)
(HAS-BLOOD A)

> (assoc 'is-located employee-1)
(IS-LOCATED IVORY-TOWER)

> (assoc 'job employee-1)
(JOB PRESIDENT)
```

```
> (assoc 'personality employee-1)
(PERSONALITY OPTIMIST)

> (assoc 'date-of-hire employee-1)
NIL
```

The a-list can be modified by adding new entries onto the front. (This is preferable to permanently altering the a-list with the destructive list functions.) The a-list is searched in order. If a key is contained in more than one sublist, only the first occurrence is returned. This allows us to associate new datum with a key that will then overshadow existing data. The old data is still present, but ignored. For example, if the employee in the example above has a change of personality, we could add a new sublist to the a-list, as follows:

```
> (setf employee-1
>      (cons '(personality pessimist) employee-1))
((PERSONALITY PESSIMIST) (JOB PRESIDENT) (HAS-BLOOD A)
   (PERSONALITY OPTIMIST) (IS-LOCATED IVORY-TOWER))

> (assoc 'personality employee-1)
(PERSONALITY PESSIMIST)

> (setf employee-1
>      (cons '(date-of-hire 84) employee-1))
((DATE-OF-HIRE 84) (PERSONALITY PESSIMIST) (JOB PRESIDENT) (HAS-BLOOD A)
   (PERSONALITY OPTIMIST) (IS-LOCATED IVORY-TOWER))

> (assoc 'date-of-hire employee-1)
(DATE-OF-HIRE 84)
```

PROPERTY LIST FUNCTIONS

Procedure	Description
GET	get the value of a property
REMPROP	remove a property
SETF	set the value of a property
SYMBOL-PLIST	show symbol's property list

Property lists (also referred to as *p-lists*) are similar to association lists: They are both composed of entries of corresponding keys and data. The difference between a property list and an association list is that a property list is directly connected to a symbol, whereas an association list may be handed around and set as the value of a symbol. A property list is composed of unique entries, whereas an association list may contain duplicate entries. The association list is usually updated by adding items to the front of the list that overshadow old entries. Updating a property list involves permanently altering the property list to reflect the new value; old values are lost.

GET

> format: (get symbol property)

SETF

> format: (setf (get symbol property) value)

GET retrieves a property value from a symbol. It returns only the value, not a list of values. The default value NIL is returned if a property does not exist on the given symbol's p-list. Therefore, a property value should never be given a NIL value. A property value is initialized using the procedure GET in combination with SETF.

Examples

```
> (setf (get 'employee-2 'job) 'assistant)
ASSISTANT
> (setf (get 'employee-2 'has-blood) 'A)
A

> (setf (get 'employee-2 'personality) 'sincere)
SINCERE

> (setf (get 'employee-2 'is-located) 'front-desk)
FRONT-DESK
```

SYMBOL-PLIST

> format: (symbol-plist symbol)

The procedure symbol-plist will return a symbol's property list.

Examples

```
> (symbol-plist 'employee-2)
(IS-LOCATED FRONT-DESK PERSONALITY SINCERE HAS-BLOOD A JOB ASSISTANT)

> (get 'employee-2 'has-blood)
A

> (get employee-2 is-located)

FRONT-DESK
> (get 'employee-2 'job)
ASSISTANT
```

```
> (get 'employee-2 'personality)
SINCERE

> (setf (get 'employee-2 'job) 'vice-president)
VICE-PRESIDENT

> (symbol-plist 'employee-2)
(IS-LOCATED FRONT-DESK PERSONALITY SINCERE HAS-BLOOD A JOB VICE-
   PRESIDENT)

> (get 'employee-2 'date-of-hire)
NIL

> (setf (get 'employee-2 'date-of-hire) 86)
86

> (symbol-plist 'employee-2)
(DATE-OF-HIRE 86 IS-LOCATED FRONT-DESK PERSONALITY SINCERE HAS-BLOOD
   A JOB VICE-PRESIDENT)
```

REMPROP

format: (remprop symbol property)

Remprop will remove a property from a symbol's p-list.

Example

```
> (remprop 'employee-2 'personality)
NIL

> (symbol-plist 'employee-2)
(DATE-OF-HIRE 86 IS-LOCATED FRONT-DESK HAS-BLOOD A JOB VICE-PRESIDENT)
```

EXERCISES

1. Write routine MATCH-BLOOD that takes two association lists as arguments and returns MATCH if both employees have the same blood type. It will return NO-MATCH if the blood types differ. Try the following cases:

```
(setf emp1 '((has-blood a) (date-of-hire 86) (personality pessimist)))
((HAS-BLOOD A) (DATE-OF-HIRE 86) (PERSONALITY PESSIMIST))

(setf emp2 '((has-blood b) (date-of-hire 86) (personality moody)))
((HAS-BLOOD B) (DATE-OF-HIRE 86) (PERSONALITY MOODY))
```

```
(setf emp3 '((has-blood a)(date-of-hire 85)(personality pessimist)))
((HAS-BLOOD A)(DATE-OF-HIRE 85)(PERSONALITY PESSIMIST))

(MATCH-BLOOD emp1 emp2)
NO-MATCH

(MATCH-BLOOD emp1 emp3)
MATCH

(MATCH-BLOOD emp2 emp3)
NO-MATCH
```

2. Write a routine VACATION that takes an association list and the current year and returns NEEDS-VACATION if the employee has been with the company at least one year and is a pessimist. It will return KEEP-WORKING otherwise. Try the following three cases based on the example above:

```
(VACATION emp1 86)
KEEP-WORKING

(VACATION emp2 86)
KEEP-WORKING

(VACATION emp3 86)
NEEDS-VACATION
```

3. Write a procedure to extract the key items from an association list of employee data. Return those items in a list.

ANSWERS

1. ```
(defun MATCH-BLOOD (patient donor)
   (cond ((equal (assoc 'has-blood patient)
                 (assoc 'has-blood donor)) 'MATCH)
         (T 'NO-MATCH)))
```
2. ```
(defun VACATION (person year)
   (if (and (>= (- year (cadr (assoc 'date-of-hire person))) 1)
            (eq 'pessimist (cadr (assoc 'personality person))))
       'needs-vacation 'keep-working))
```
3. ```
(defun EXTRACT (L)
   (setf keys '())
   (dolist (elt L keys)
       (setf keys (cons (car elt) (keys)))))
```
```

14

Destructive List Functions

Procedure	Description
NCONC	permanently merge lists
RPLACA	permanently replace CAR (first element) on list
RPLACD	permanently replace CDR (all except first element) of the list
DELETE	permanently delete occurrences of an element on a list

Most of the functions used to manipulate list structure that we have examined thus far (CONS, APPEND, SUBST, and so forth) do not permanently change existing list structure, but only create new ones or make modifications by copying arguments. LISP provides functions that can permanently alter the structure of lists. They should be used with extreme caution, because *you may obtain unexpected results if a list is shared and altered by different functions*. (If you are a novice, you may want to skip this section.)

You have seen that the function SETF can permanently change the elments on a list. The functions presented here—NCONC, RPLACA, and RPLACD—are special cases of the SETF function. When used with care, the destructive list functions can optimize your use of lists by replacing elements on a list, rather than making modifications by copying arguments and returning the copies.

CONCATENATING LISTS

NCONC

format: (nconc list-expr1 . . . list-exprn)

The NCONC function appears to be similar to the APPEND function. The results generated by both these functions appear to be the same. The difference is that the NCONC function permanently alters the list by physically changing the value of list-expr1 to be a merge of itself with all succeeding arguments. The value returned from the NCONC function is the concatenation of list-expr1 through list-exprn. The APPEND function returns a copy of the merged lists and does not alter any of its arguments. The following examples demonstrate the difference between the APPEND function and the NCONC function:

Examples

```
> (setf a (list 'I 'AM 'MERGED))
(I AM MERGED)

> (setf b (list 'TEMPORARILY))
(TEMPORARILY)

> (setf c (list 'PERMANENTLY))
(PERMANENTLY)

> (append a b)
(I AM MERGED TEMPORARILY)

> a
(I AM MERGED)                   ;value of a is unchanged

> b
(TEMPORARILY)                   ;value of b is unchanged

> (nconc a c)
(I AM MERGED PERMANENTLY)

> a
(I AM MERGED PERMANENTLY)       ;value of a is permanently altered

> c
(PERMANENTLY)                   ;value of c is unchanged
```

REPLACING LIST ELEMENTS

RPLACA

format: (rplaca list-expr elt)

The RPLACA function alters a list by replacing the first element on the list with the second argument passed to the function. It permanently replaces the CAR of the list with a new element.

Examples

```
> (setf a '(spring summer fall))
(SPRING SUMMER FALL)

> (rplaca a 'winter)
(WINTER SUMMER FALL)

> a
(WINTER SUMMER FALL)

> (rplaca a '(the seasons))
((THE SEASONS) SUMMER FALL)

> a
((THE SEASONS) SUMMER FALL)

> (rplaca (car a) 2)
(2 SEASONS)
```

RPLACD

format: (rplacd list-expr list-expr1)

The RPLACD function alters a list by replacing everything but the first element on the list with the second list argument to the function. It permanently replaces the CDR of the list with a new list. Only the first element (the CAR) of the list being operated on remains unchanged.

Examples

```
> (setf b '(winter spring))
(WINTER SPRING)

> (rplacd a b)
((2 SEASONS) WINTER SPRING)
```

```
> a
((2 SEASONS) WINTER SPRING)

> (rplacd a '(salt pepper))
((2 SEASONS) SALT PEPPER)

> a
((2 SEASONS) SALT PEPPER)

> (rplacd (car a) '(spices))
(2 SPICES)

> a
((2 SPICES) SALT PEPPER)
```

REMOVING LIST ELEMENTS

DELETE

format: (delete elt list-expr)

The DELETE function permanently removes all occurrences of an element from a list. The list is altered to consist of the original list without any deleted elements. A peculiarity of this function is that the function returns the list without the deleted elements, except that an element at the head of the list will not be deleted. In order to permanently delete an element at the head of the list, the function SETF should be used to reinitialize the list to the value returned from the DELETE function.

Examples

```
> (setf a '(1 2 3 1 2 3))
(1 2 3 1 2 3)

> (delete 2 a)
(1 3 1 3)

> a
(1 3 1 3)
```

The function SETF must be used to reinitialize the list whenever you want to delete the first element on a list.

```
> (setf list1 '(head tail))
(HEAD TAIL)
```

```
> (delete 'head list1)
(TAIL)

> list1
(HEAD TAIL)

> (setf list1 (delete 'head list1))
(TAIL)

> list1
(TAIL)
```

15

File I/O Functions

Function	Description
OPENI	open a file for input (read only)
OPENO	open a file for output (write only)
CLOSE	close a file

The following functions access the contents of a file.

Function	Description
READ-CHAR	return a character from a file
PEEK-CHAR	display the next character in the file, skip if space
WRITE-CHAR	write a character to a file
READ-LINE	return a line from a file

XLISP has very limited file-accessing functions. You have two file open options: OPENI opens a file for input only, and OPENO opens a file for output only. The general Common LISP function OPEN does not exist in XLISP. Some concepts must be established before proceeding with a description of the I/O functions.

A DISCUSSION ON FILE POINTERS AND FILE POSITION

The file I/O functions OPENI and OPENO return a unique file pointer for each file opened. A *file pointer* is only a handle on an internal representation of a file. This file pointer is in the format #<File: #nnnn>, where nnnn is a unique number for each file accessed. The file cannot be accessed by directly typing in this value, since it is only a representation. Therefore, a symbol must be initialized to the file pointer in order to access it with any of the file I/O functions.

For purposes of discussion in this tutorial, the term *file pointer* must be distinguished from the term *file position*. When a file is opened, the file position points to the first character in the file and advances sequentially through the file. The file position always points to the next character to be accessed. There is no function in XLISP to reposition the file position within the file. The file position cannot be "backed up" within the file or advanced more than one character or line at a time through the file.

OPENI

format: (openi file-name-string)

The function OPENI allows you to open a system file for read only. The file must exist, and the argument name must be a string, i.e., between double quotes. The function returns a file pointer that must be saved as the value of a symbol. If the file does not exist, the symbol NIL is returned. The file position is initialized to the beginning of the file; that is, it points to the first character. Note that only read functions are valid on files that have been opened with the OPENI function. Any output functions used are invalid even though using them does not generate an error; the data you think you are writing will not be saved back to the original file. The format for saving the file pointer as a symbol is

(setf file-ptr-elt (openi file-name-string))

OPENO

format: (openo file-name-string)

The function OPENO allows you to open a system file for output. The argument name must be a string, i.e., between double quotes. The function returns a file pointer that must be saved as a symbol. This function creates the file if it does not exist. *If the file already exists, its current contents will be lost, and it will be treated as a newly created file.* You should take care when opening files for output that you do not inadvertently destroy files. Since the file is opened for output, the file position always points to the beginning of an empty file. Note that only write functions are valid on files that have been opened with the OPENO function. Any read functions used will simply return NIL, since the file position is always pointing to the end of the file. The format for saving the file pointer as a symbol is

```
(setf file-ptr-elt (openo file-name-string))
```

CLOSE

```
format: (close file-ptr-elt)
```

The CLOSE function closes a file that has been opened with OPENO or OPENI. The file pointer element symbol name that you saved as a handle to the file is used as the argument to close the file. The value NIL is returned. An invalid file pointer argument generates an error. Once a file has been closed, it cannot be accessed until another open command is issued.

ACCESSING THE FILE

The following functions allow you to access a file, that is, to read the contents of or write to a file.

READ-CHAR

```
format: (read-char file-ptr-elt)
```

The function READ-CHAR reads the character in the file from where the file position is pointing. It will be returned to you as its ASCII value. The file position advances to point to the next character in the file. The symbol NIL is returned at end of file. A file opened with the OPENO function cannot be read; the function READ-CHAR always returns NIL when trying to read a newly created file, since the file position always points to the end of the file.

PEEK-CHAR

```
format: (peek-char space-flag file-ptr-elt)
```

The function PEEK-CHAR returns the character in the file from where the file pointer is positioned. It returns it to you as its ASCII value. The file position does not advance to point to the next character in the file unless the character matches the character specified in the space-flag. The symbol NIL is returned at the end of file. This function can be used to check for special characters in a file and skip over them. For example, the space-flag can be initialized to skip over white space or punctuation marks.

WRITE-CHAR

```
format: (write-char ascii-value file-ptr-elt)
```

The function WRITE-CHAR writes a character to the file where the file position is pointing. The argument specifying the character must be its ASCII value. It returns the character equivalent. The file must have been opened for output with the function OPENO in order for the write to be valid. Although the WRITE-CHAR function does not generate an error when writing to a file opened with the OPENI function, the characters written will not be saved back to the original file.

READ-LINE

```
format: (read-line file-ptr-elt)
```

The function READ-LINE reads the entire line in the file from where the file position is pointing. (A *line* is any string of characters terminated by <return>.) It returns the line as a string of characters. The file position advances to point to the next line in the file. The symbol NIL is returned at end of file.

Examples

1. Create the file "testread.doc" with your text editor and input the following two lines of text, terminating each line with <return>:

   ```
   2 lines
   of text
   ```

   Close the file and start the interpreter. The following functions will demonstrate how to read a file.

```
> (setf fp (openi "testread.doc"))  ; open file for input only
#<File: #nnnn>

> (read-char fp)                    ; return ASCII value
                                      representing "2" and
                                    ; advance file position 1 character

50

> (peek-char " " fp)                ; skip next character if  a space
108

> (read-char fp)                    ; advance past
                                      next character, letter "l"

108
```

```
> (string (read-char fp))          ;read character and convert ASCII
                                    ;value to a character string
"i"

> (read-line fp)                   ;return rest of line as a string of
                                    ;characters and advance file
                                    ;position to next line
"nes"

> (read-line fp)                   ;return line as a string
                                      of characters and
                                    ;advance  file position to next line
"of text"

> (read-line fp)                   ;read next line, NIL indicates EOF
NIL

> (close fp)
NIL
```

Note the use of the function STRING in this example and the function CHAR in the next example. These functions are very useful when reading and writing a file, since they can convert characters to ASCII values, and ASCII values to characters.

2. To write a file,

```
> (setf fo (openo "testwrit.doc"))    ;open file for output only
#<File: #nnnn>

> (write-char (char "A" 0) fo)        ;write character "A" and
                                      ;advance file position
                                      ;return ASCII value of "A"
65

> (string (write-char 65 fo))         ;write character "A" and
                                      ;advance file position
                                      ;return character value of
ASCII
                                      ;code 65
"A"

> (write-char (char "b" 0) fo)        ;write character "b" and
                                      ;advance file position
                                      ;return ASCII value of "b"
98
```

```
> (write-char (char "\n" 0) fo)          ;write newline character and
                                         ;advance file position
                                         ;return ASCII value of"\n"
10

> (write-char (char "0" 0) fo)           ;write character "0" and
                                         ;advance file position
                                         ;return ASCII value of "0"
48

> (write-char (char "9" 0) fo)           ;write character "9" and
                                         ;advance file position
                                         ;return ASCII value  of "9"
57

> (close fo)                             ;close the file
NIL
```

If you examine the file ''testwrit.doc,'' it contains the following characters:

AAb
09

16

Print and Read Functions

Function	Description
(Standard I/O)	
READ	read from standard input (the terminal)
PRINT	print to standard output (the terminal) with line feed
PRIN1	print to standard output (the terminal) (no line feed)
(Accessing a File)	
PRINT	print to a file (with line feed)
PRIN1	print to a file (no line feed)
READ	read from a file
FLATSIZE	return length of expression (as printed)
(Formatting a File)	
PRINC	print with no line feed or string delimiters
TERPRI	terminate this line, start a new line
FLATC	return length of expression with no string delimiters

The PRINT and READ functions give you several options. They allow you to inter-
act through the terminal with the interpreter (standard I/O) and also to create and read
files. These files can be formatted with print commands so that they can be read as data by
the XLISP interpreter or as text by a user.

READING FROM STANDARD INPUT
AND PRINTING TO STANDARD OUTPUT

READ

```
format: (read)
```

The READ function accepts input from you from standard input, the terminal. The interpreter stops and waits for you to type something followed by <return>.

```
> (setf x (read))        ; the interpreter waits for a response

>10                      ; you type in 10 followed by <return>
10

> x                      ; x is bound to value typed in
10
```

After executing the READ function, the interpreter waits forever for you to type in a response. Therefore, it is always useful to precede the READ function with the PRINT function, which informs you as to what type of response it is expecting.

PRINT AND PRIN1

```
formats: (print arg) and (prin1 arg)
```

The PRINT and PRIN1 functions print the argument to you at the terminal, standard output. The PRINT function outputs its argument followed by a newline character. The PRIN1 function prints its argument with no linefeed. Note that the argument is printed twice. The first response is a result of the PRINT function writing its argument to the terminal, and the second response is the interpreter displaying the result of the last function executed, which is the PRINT function.

```
> (print x)          ; PRINT example
10
10

> (prin1 x)          ; PRIN1 example
1010

> (print 'HELLO)     ; PRINT example
HELLO
HELLO

> (prin1 'HELLO)     ; PRIN1 example
HELLOHELLO
```

Within a user-defined function the PRINT function can be used to prompt you, and using the READ function, the response you type in can be bound to a symbol. Since the READ function waits forever for your response, it is always a good idea to precede any READ statement with a PRINT statement indicating to the user what type of response is expected. (See the integer-averaging example in Chapter 11.)

READING FROM AND PRINTING TO A FILE

In order to be accessed, a file must be opened with the proper command, OPENI for read and OPENO for print.

PRINT AND PRIN1

```
formats:  (print arg optional-fileptr)
          (prin1 arg optional-fileptr)
```

PRINT and PRIN1 output their arguments to the file exactly as the arguments appear. The difference between the functions is that PRINT outputs its argument followed by the newline character; PRIN1 does not insert the newline character. These functions are useful when writing to files that will later be read as input files by the XLISP interpreter, since data types will be printed in the format the READ function expects.

```
> (setf fo (openo "test.doc"))          ;create an output file
#<File: #nnnn>

> (print "i am a string" fo)            ;write a string to the file
"i am a string"

> (print 99 fo)                         ;write an integer to the file
99

> (print '(elt1 elt2) fo)               ;write a list to the file
(ELT1 ELT2)

> (prin1 "these strings will appear" fo)   ;PRIN1 example
"these strings will appear"

> (prin1 "on the same line" fo)         ;there will be no line feed
"on the same line"

> (close fo)
NIL
```

If you examine file "test.doc," it will contain the following text:

```
"i am a string"
99
(ELT1 ELT2)
"these strings will appear""on the same line"
```

READ

```
               format: (read optional-fileptr optional-eof)
```

The READ function returns the next expression within the file. The file position is
advanced past special characters, such as the space and the end-of-line characters. The
default NIL is returned at end-of-file, unless the optional-eof parameter is used.

```
> (setf fi (openi "test.doc"))        ;open file for read
#<File: #nnnn>

> (read fi)                           ;return the string
"i am a string"

> (read fi)                           ;return the integer value
99

> (read fi)                           ;return the list
(ELT1 ELT2)

> (read fi)                           ;return first string on the line
"these strings will appear"

> (read fi)                           ;return next string, same line
"on the same line"

> (read fi)                           ;return end-of-file, default is NIL
NIL

> (close fi)                          ;close file
NIL
```

NIL is the default end-of-file parameter returned to you. An optional parameter can
be specified to return a value at end-of-file. In this example, symbols are bound to the
values from each read.

```
> (setf fi (openi "test.doc"))          ;open file for read
#<File: #nnnn>

> (setf string-sym (read fi 'EOF))
"i am a string"
```

```
> (setf int-sym (read fi 'EOF))
99

> (setf list-sym (read fi 'EOF))
(ELT1 ELT2)

> (setf string-sym1 (read fi 'EOF))
"these strings will appear"

> (setf string-sym2 (read fi 'EOF))
"on the same line"

> (read fi 'EOF)                        ;return end-of-file
EOF

> (close fi)                            ;close file
NIL
```

FLATSIZE

format: (flatsize expr)

The FLATSIZE function returns the numeric length of an expression that includes all characters in the expression that would be printed. Note that this includes the double quotes in a string expression.

```
> string-sym
"i am a string"

> (flatsize string-sym)
15

> int-sym
99

> (flatsize int-sym)
2

> list-sym
(ELT1 ELT2)

> (flatsize list-sym)
11
```

FORMATTING A FILE

The following functions are useful when you want to format an output file for a person to read (as opposed to the functions noted above, which are useful when the files are to be read by the XLISP READ function). These functions strip the string delimiters off of strings and may ignore other special characters.

PRINC

format: (princ arg optional-fileptr)

PRINC is similar to PRIN1 except that it ignores the double quotes around string elements. This allows you to put text from strings into an output file without the string delimiters.

```
> (setf fo (openo "test.doc"))              ;open file for output
#<File: #nnnn>

> (princ "these strings will appear " fo)    ;write a string
"these strings will appear "

> (princ "on the same line " fo)             ;write a string
"on the same line "

> (princ "without the quotes" fo)            ;write a string
"without the quotes."

> (close fo)
NIL
```

The file you have just written contains the following text:

```
            These strings will appear
            on the same line
            without the quotes.
```

TERPRI

format: (terpri optional-fileptr)

The TERPRI function terminates the current print line, that is, generates a new line. It gives you control of where to insert new lines, particularly when using the PRINC or PRIN1 commands.

```
> (setf fo (openo "test.doc"))              ;open file for output
#<File: #nnnn>

> (princ "these strings will appear" fo)     ;write a string
"these strings will appear"

> (terpri fo)                                ;insert new line
NIL
```

```
> (princ "on different lines" fo)                ;write a string
"on different lines"

> (terpri fo)                                    ;insert new line
NIL

> (princ "without the quotes" fo)               ;write a string
"without the quotes"

> (terpri fo)                                    ;insert new line
NIL

> (close fo)
NIL
```

The file you have just written will contain the following text:

```
These strings will appear
on different lines
without the quotes
```

FLATC

```
format: (flatc expr)
```

The FLATC function returns the numeric length of an expression that includes all characters in the expression that would be printed using PRINC. String delimiters are not counted.

```
> (flatc "abc")
3

> (flatc "i am a string")
13

> (flatc 99)
2

> (flatc '(elt1 elt2))
11
```

EXERCISES

1. Write the procedure ON-THE-LIST that prompts the user for a symbol. If the symbol is on the list (peach pear plum), the message ALREADY-PRESENT is returned and the user is prompted for the next symbol. If the element is not on the list, the user is asked if they would like it put on

the list. If so, the item is appended to the list. The user is again prompted for another symbol. A response of NIL ends the session, and the new list of elements is returned.

2. Assume that the payment on a $100,000 mortgage (at 9½ percent interest for 30 years) is $841.00. For each additional $1000 financed, there is an additional payment of $8.41. Write the procedure MORTGAGE that takes as its arguments a range of values and an increment. Print a double column of information with headings as follows:

(MORTGAGE 100000 120000 5000)

Mortgage	Payment
$100000	$ 841.00
$105000	$ 883.05
$110000	$ 925.10
$115000	$ 967.15
$120000	$1009.20

3. Rewrite the procedure MORTGAGE that takes the data from Exercise 2 and writes it to a file, which is also passed as an argument:

(MTGE-FILE 100000 120000 5000 "payments")

The file "payments" contains the data printed to the terminal in Exercise 2.

ANSWERS

1.
```
(defun ON-THE-LIST (&aux sym fruit)
      (do ((sym T) (fruit '(peach pear plum)))
          ((eq sym NIL) fruit)
          (print "ENTER SYMBOL NAME")
          (setf sym (read))
          (cond ((eq sym NIL))  ;end the session
                ((member sym fruit) (print 'ALREADY-PRESENT))
                (T (print "PUT IT ON THE LIST?")  ;default
                   (if (not (eq (read) NIL))
                       (setf fruit (append (list sym) fruit)))))))
```

2.
```
(defun MORTGAGE (start-val end-val increment)
    (princ "MORTGAGE      PAYMENT")
    (terpri)
    (do ((start start-val (+ start increment)))
        ((> start end-val) 'done)
        (princ "$")
        (prin1 start)
        (princ "      $")
        (print (CALCULATE start))))

(defun CALCULATE (val)
    (+ 841.0 (* 8.41 (/ (- val 100000) 1000))))
```

3.
```
(defun MTGE-FILE (start-val end-val increment file &aux fn)
    (setf fn (openo file))
    (princ "MORTGAGE        PAYMENT" fn)
    (terpri fn)
    (do ((start start-val (+ start increment)))
        ((> start end-val))
        (princ "$" fn)
        (prin1 start fn)
        (princ "        $" fn)
        (print (CALCULATE start) fn))

    (close fn)
    (print 'DONE))
```

17

Debugging and Error Handling

Function	Description
ERROR	signal a non-correctable error
CERROR	signal a correctable error
BREAK	enter a break loop
BAKTRACE	print levels of traceback information

SYSTEM-GENERATED ERROR MESSAGES

You have probably generated more than a few errors when typing in the XLISP examples in this tutorial. As described in Chapter 1, if the system parameter *breakenable* was set to NIL, the interpreter would ignore the error and keep processing. If *breakenable* was set to T, the interpreter entered you into the error handler. You entered either (clean-up) or <control-Z> to exit to the previous level, or <control-C> to return to the top level. This allowed you to retry the function without actually being aware of how to analyze and correct the problem.

The modified prompt actually signaled that you had generated an error and put you in the debugger, which allows you to analyze the cause of the problem by using any of the XLISP functions available to you. For example, you could show variable bindings, execute other XLISP functions, trace back through the series of statements executed before the error was generated, and so forth.

You have probably noticed two different error message formats generated by the XLISP interpreter. The first format simply states the error messsage, followed by the error prompt. The second format states the error condition, followed by the message "if continued: (some message)." The first format signals that you have generated a fatal and noncorrectable error, and the latter format allows you a chance to correct the error and continue processing from that point. Typing the function CONTINUE tells the interpreter you have attempted to fix the problem and wish to proceed. You cannot continue from a fatal error. These simple examples demonstrate the two error formats.

Examples

1. Fatal error

```
> (abs 1 2)
error: too many arguments  -  (ABS 1 2)

1:> (clean-up)                              ;a fatal error has
                                            ;been generated

[abort to previous level]
>
```

2. Correctable error

```
> a                                         ;a is an unbound symbol
error: unbound variable > A
if continued: try evaluating symbol again

1:> (setf a 2)                              ;you can correct the error
2

1:> (continue)                              ;the function CONTINUE
                                            ;allows you to retry
[continue from break loop]
2
```

USER-GENERATED ERROR MESSAGES

You can use the same error functions within your user-defined functions. They are especially useful for providing error messages to the user of your program. The formats are given below.

ERROR

```
        formats:  (error message) and (error message print-arg)
```

The ERROR function signals a noncorrectable error. A noncorrectable error is a fatal error. The interpreter enters the debugger, allowing you to determine the cause of the error, but does not allow you to continue.

The first argument to this function allows you to print a message to the user that should accurately describe the error. This message must be a string. The optional argument expression allows you to print the value of a variable after the error message or any expression.

The following example verifies if a number is within the valid range of zero through nine. It generates a fatal error if not.

```
> (defun SIGNAL-ERROR (x)
1> (if (and (>= x 0) (< x 10)) (print "NUMBER WITHIN RANGE")
2>      (error "NUMBER MUST BE IN RANGE 0 THRU 9 ** YOU ENTERED" x)))

SIGNAL-ERROR

> (SIGNAL-ERROR 1)
""NUMBER WITHIN RANGE''

> (SIGNAL-ERROR 11)
error: NUMBER MUST BE IN RANGE 0 THRU 9 ** YOU ENTERED - 11

1:> (clean-up)
[abort to previous level]
>
```

CERROR

formats: (cerror message emessage) and (cerror message emessage print-arg)

The CERROR function signals a correctable error. A correctable error puts you in the debugger and also allows you to continue. The first argument is the message that is printed after the "if continued" statement, notifying the user what is expected if the function is to be continued without generating further errors. The next argument is the message that is printed following "error:" and should be an accurate description of the error. All message arguments must be strings. The optional argument expression allows you to print the value of the variable in error after the error message.

The following example demonstrates the CERROR function within a loop, allowing the verification of each subsequent value that a user enters. When a valid value is entered, the user can continue the execution of the interpreter by entering the function CONTINUE.

```
> (defun SIGNAL-CERR (x)
1> (do ()
2>       ((and (>= x 0) (< x 10)) (print "NUMBER WITHIN RANGE"))
2>          (cerror "NUMBER MUST BE IN RANGE 0 THRU 9"
3>                 "NUMBER OUT OF RANGE ** YOU ENTERED" x)))
SIGNAL-CERR
```

```
> (setf x 11)
11


> (SIGNAL-CERR x)
error: NUMBER OUT OF RANGE ** YOU ENTERED - 11
if continued: NUMBER MUST BE IN RANGE 0 THRU 9


1:> (setf x 80)                        ;you inadvertently enter
                                       ;another incorrect value
80


1:> (continue)
[continue from break loop]
error: NUMBER OUT OF RANGE ** YOU ENTERED - 80
if continued: NUMBER MUST BE IN RANGE 0 THRU 9


1:> (setf x 8)
8


1:> (continue)
"NUMBER WITHIN RANGE"
```

DEBUGGING TOOLS

BREAK

```
formats: (break), (break message), and (break message print-arg)
```

The BREAK function is similar to the CERROR function. It stops execution of the program and prints an optional message and an optional variable value. It is useful for setting breakpoints when debugging programs. The CONTINUE function allows you to continue processing.

```
> (break)
break:


1:> (continue)
[continue from break loop]
NIL


> (break "STOP")              ;user-defined message
break: STOP


1:> (continue)
NIL


> (setf b 99)
99
```

```
> (break "VALUE OF b" b)            ;user-defined message and variable value
break: VALUE OF b - 99

1:> (continue)
[continue from break loop]
NIL
>
```

This function determines if an overflow condition will occur when a number is squared. (On the IBM PC, the range of valid integer values is $-2,147,483,648$ through $2,147,483,647$.)

```
> (defun SQUARE (x)
1>     (if (or (< x -46340)(> x 46340))
2>             (break "OVERFLOW IF SQUARED" x))
1>     (* x x))
SQUARE

> (SQUARE 46340)
2147395600

> (SQUARE 46341)
break: OVERFLOW IF SQUARED - 46341

1:> (continue)                       ;produces an incorrect answer
[continue from break loop]
-2147479015

> (SQUARE -46340)
2147395600

> (SQUARE -46341)
break: OVERFLOW IF SQUARED - -46341

1:> (continue)                       ;produces an incorrect answer
[continue from break loop]
>2147479015
```

BAKTRACE

formats: (baktrace) and (baktrace num)

The BAKTRACE function allows you to trace the steps in reverse order that have occurred up to the point that an error was generated. The optional number argument allows you to specify how many levels to trace and display. This function is useful when debugging, as the order of evaluation of statements in reverse order can be shown.

The following function has an error in the last clause of the COND function and will generate an error when the interpreter tries to execute the statement.

```
>  (defun FARM (x)
1>      (cond ((= x "cat")   'MEOW)
2>             ((= x "dog")   'BARK)
2>             ((= x "rat")   'EEEK)
2>             ((= x goat)   'BLEAT)))
FARM


>  (FARM "cat")
MEOW
MEOW


>  (FARM "rat")
EEEK
EEEK


>  (FARM "goat")
error: unbound variable — GOAT
if continued: try evaluating symbol again
```

At this point, you can use the BAKTRACE function to determine where the error occurred. You can see that the unbound symbol goat is displayed first, then the predicate function " = " referencing the unbound symbol, and then the entire COND function containing the predicate function. Finally, the actual function call is displayed followed by the symbol NIL, signifying top-level.

```
1:>  (baktrace)
(BAKTRACE)
GOAT
(= X GOAT)
(COND ((= X "CAT") (QUOTE MEOW)) ((= X "DOG") (QUOTE BARK)) ((= X "RAT")
(QUOTE EEEK)) ((= X GOAT)  (QUOTE BLEAT)))
(FARM "GOAT")
NIL
```

You can also trace back a specified number of levels:

```
1:>  (baktrace 3)
(BAKTRACE 3)
GOAT
(= X GOAT)
NIL
1:>  (clean-up)
```

At this point, you should practice using the error-handling mechanism. Fluency in using the error-handling mechanism can provide you with a lot of useful information that can save you time when you are beginning to write programs.

18

Memory Management Functions

Function	Description
GC	force garbage collection
MEM	show memory allocation statistics
EXPAND	expand memory by adding segments
ALLOC	change number of nodes to allocate in each segment

GC (GARBAGE COLLECTION)

format: (gc)

The XLISP interpreter assigns memory cells automatically when you need them from a list of memory cells known as the *free storage list*. These memory cells can then be accessed as structures within the system. For example, when you create a list, a memory cell is assigned for each element of the list.

Since we have the ability to mutate internal pointers to these memory cells using various XLISP functions, memory cells that were previously in use can be lost and are known as "garbage." The DELETE function is an example of a function that creates garbage when it deletes elements off a list. If enough of these no-longer-used memory cells are generated, they will eventually use up all your available memory space and stop the interpreter entirely. They must somehow be recycled and restored to the free storage list.

This recycling process is known as *garbage collection*. Executing the function GC restores the pointers to the unused cells to the free storage list. Garbage collection can be performed at any time, but will be most useful after you have done a lot of list manipulations. XLISP will also automatically invoke the garbage collection function for you when it runs out of memory. The function GC will always return NIL.

```
>  (gc)
NIL
```

MEM

```
format  (mem)
```

The MEM function shows the memory allocation statistics currently in use by the XLISP interpreter. Shown are some sample values:

```
>  (mem)
Nodes: 1000          ; number of nodes (cells) allocated
Free nodes: 57       ; number of nodes (cells) in the free storage list
Segments: 1          ; number of segments allocated
Allocate: 1000       ; number of nodes to allocate in each segment
Total: 7004          ; total number of bytes of memory in use
Collections: 1       ; number of garbage collections
NIL
>
```

EXPAND

```
format:  (expand num)
```

The EXPAND function expands the memory available to the XLISP interpreter by adding the specified number of memory segments. The actual number of segments added is returned. Memory is expanded whenever the initialization code runs out of space.

```
>  (expand 1)
1
```

ALLOC

```
format:  (alloc num)
```

The ALLOC function changes the number of nodes to allocate in each segment. The argument indicates the new number of nodes, and the function returns the former number of nodes allocated. The default number of nodes is 1000 for the IBM PC.

```
> (alloc 1500)
1000

> (alloc 2000)
1500
```

19

Recursion

Recursion is a programming technique, rather than a LISP function. Free use of recursion makes LISP interesting because of the great power that can be derived from it. It is presented in great detail here since many novice programmers have trouble understanding it. Most functions written recursively can be written nonrecursively.

Experienced LISP programmers like to use recursion because of its power and because it often provides an elegant solution to a problem. Functions written recursively tend to be much shorter. They are easier to understand since there is less to look at.

The procedures we have discussed so far in this manual have consisted of sequential processing, conditional expressions, and iterative functions. This section of the tutorial deals with the class of functions that are recursive in nature.

Most programmers have experience with programming languages where the flow of control is straightforward. In FORTRAN and PASCAL, you design the program so that subroutines are called to carry out clearly defined tasks. The main program calls the subroutine, it is executed, and control is returned to the main routine. If the subroutine is called from within a loop, it may be executed many times, but each call transfers control out of the main routine.

In LISP, we can also design programs in this manner. Examples have already been presented of procedures that use sequential (the PROG procedures) and iterative constructs (the DO procedures). LISP also gives us the option to define recursive procedures, procedures that call upon themselves to execute subtasks. Recursion is most often used when analyzing expressions on lists of unknown or variable length and in the computation of mathematical values.

In order to implement a recursive procedure, the task must be capable of being broken into two cases: (1) the trivial or terminating case and (2) the general case. A recursive function will then call *itself* to perform the subtasks associated with each case and will terminate when the problem has been simplified to its trivial case.

It is often very difficult for programmers familiar with traditional programming methods to think recursively. It is a concept that must be learned. The following examples attempt to explain the method in a simple manner.

MATHEMATICAL PROBLEMS

Many mathematical problems can be defined recursively. Arithmetic and geometric progressions are easily defined in terms of recursion. A *progression* is any sequence of numbers, each of which, after the first, is obtained by adding or multiplying the preceding number by a constant number. Many everyday problems can be defined in terms of progressions.

The examples below are presented as word problems, which most of you are familiar with from other mathematics classes. Hopefully this will help you understand recursion, which can then be applied to these and other problems. (Note that in the real world, recursion may not be the best way to implement some of these solutions.)

The following procedure is a simple example demonstrating recursion. The procedure RECURSE calls itself x times and returns the value of the argument passed to the procedure. It essentially does nothing.

```
(defun RECURSE (x)
1>      (cond ((zerop x) 0)              ;terminating condition
2>            (T (1+ (RECURSE (1- x))))))) ;descend
RECURSE

>  (RECURSE 3)
3
```

Tracing through the example for $x = 3$, we get

```
RECURSE(3), descend
        RECURSE(2), descend
                RECURSE(1), descend
                        RECURSE(0), terminate
                        RECURSE returns 0, ascend
                RECURSE returns 1, ascend
        RECURSE returns 2, ascend
RECURSE returns 3, finished
```

We have effectively created

$$\text{RECURSE (3)} = (1 + (1 + (1 + 0)))$$

Note that each recursive call makes demands on the available system memory. Therefore, when you try to nest many levels of recursion beyond what the system can handle, the following error message will appear:

```
error: evaluation stack overflow
```

Examples

1. Almost everyone is familiar with the probability of obtaining heads when flipping a coin. On any one given flip, the probability is 0.5. The probability of obtaining heads on two flips is 0.5 * 0.5, of obtaining heads three times given three flips is 0.5 * 0.5 * 0.5, and so forth. We can define a recursive function that will tell us the probability of obtaining heads for x flips of the coin. The following is a restatement of the problem:

Simple case: $x = 0$, return 1
Other cases: $x >= 1$, return $0.5 * 0.5^{x-1}$

Translating the cases into LISP:

Simple case: (defun FLIP (coin) (cond ((zerop coin) 1)))
Other cases: (defun FLIP (coin) (* 0.5 (FLIP (1 − coin))))

Putting the two cases together, we have the following procedure:

```
> (defun FLIP (coin)
1>      (cond ((zerop coin) 1)
2>            (T (* 0.5 (FLIP (1− coin)))))))
FLIP

> (FLIP 0)        ;returns 1
1

> (FLIP 1)        ; (* 0.5 1)
0.500000

> (FLIP 2)        ; (* 0.5 (* 0.5 1))
0.250000

> (FLIP 3)        ; (* 0.5 (* 0.5 (* 0.5 1)))
0.125000

> (FLIP 4)        ; (* 0.5 (* 0.5 (* 0.5 (* 0.5 1))))
0.062500
```

2. The number of students attending a certain college is projected to increase at a rate of 5 percent each year. If the college currently has 1000 students, what will be the percentage increase in the student population after *x* years? The procedure takes as its argument the number of years and returns the projected number of students. The problem can be restated as follows:

Simple case:	if years = 0, then return 1000
Other cases:	if years > 0, then return $1000 * 1.05^{years}$

Translating the cases into LISP, we get:

Simple case:	(defun ESTIMATED-POP (years) (cond ((zerop years) 1000)))
Other cases:	(defun ESTIMATED-POP (years)
	(* 1.05 (ESTIMATED-POP (1 − years))))

Putting the two cases together, we have the following procedure:

```
> (defun ESTIMATED-POP (years)
1>     (cond ((zerop years) 1000)
2>           (T (* 1.05 (ESTIMATED-POP (1- years))))))
ESTIMATED-POP

> (ESTIMATED-POP 3)    ; (* 1.05 (* 1.05 (* 1.05 1000)))
1157.62

> (ESTIMATED-POP 5)    ; (* 1.05 (* 1.05 (* 1.05 (* 1.05 (* 1.05 1000)))))
1276.28
```

EXERCISES

1. Write a procedure SAVINGS that takes as its argument a number of days. It will compute the amount of money you will save if you start saving $1 the first day, $2 the second day, and so forth, until you find the accumulated sum for the given amount of days.

2. You are given a standard deck of 52 cards. You are to draw a card from the deck and replace it before the next card is drawn. Write a procedure HEARTS that takes as its argument the number of cards drawn and returns the probability that all the cards drawn are hearts.

3. You invest $1000 at an annual interest rate of 5 percent per year. Write a procedure RATE that takes as its argument the number of years you leave your money in the bank and returns the amount of money accumulated.

ANSWERS

```
1. Simple case: if days = 0, return 0
   Other cases: if days = x return x + (x − 1) + (x − 2) . . . + (x − x)
```

```
(defun SAVINGS (days)
      (cond ((zerop days) 0)
            (T (+ days (SAVINGS (1- days)))))))
```
2. (defun HEARTS (cards)
```
      (cond ((zerop cards) 1)
            (T (* 0.25 (HEARTS (1- cards))))))))
```
3. (defun RATE (years)
```
      (cond ((zerop years) 1000)
            (T (* 1.05 (RATE (1- years)))))))))
```

LISTS

A common use of recursion is for evaluating expressions on a list. Since a list can have a variable number of elements on it, and the type of these elements can also vary, recursion can be quite useful as a control structure for processing the expressions on a list. The terminating condition for processing a list is when all the elements of the list have been processed; only the null list is left.

The LISP built-in procedures APPEND, LAST, ASSOC, MEMBER, and LENGTH can be defined in terms of recursion. We can use recursion to evaluate expressions at all levels of a list, not just the top-level. These are just a few of the many examples of using recursion on lists.

Let us define a simple function that will determine if all the elements on a list are numbers. The procedure NUMBERS takes a list as its argument. it will return T if all the expressions on the list are numbers, and NIL otherwise. The problem can be restated as follows:

Simple case:	null L, return T
Number cases:	(numberp (car L))(numberp (cadr L)) . . . .
	(numberp (cadd . . . ddr L)
Other cases:	return NIL

Translating the cases into LISP, we get:

Simple case:	(defun NUMBERS (L) (cond ((null L) T)))
Number cases:	(defun NUMBERS (L)
	(cond (numberp (car L))(NUMBERS (cdr L))))
Other cases:	(defun NUMBERS (L) NIL)

We can now define our routine:

```
> (defun NUMBERS (L)
1>      (cond ((null L) T)
2>            ((numberp (car L)) (NUMBERS (cdr L)))
2>            (T NIL)))
NUMBERS
```

The first condition tested for is the null list. This tells us that we have reached the end of the list and no nonnumeric items were found. (If you were to actually use this procedure, it would be necessary to make sure that the list you are passing as the argument is nonNIL, because the procedure evaluates to T for null lists.) The second condition tests for numbers, and the last condition evaluates to NIL for all other expressions, such as symbols, lists, or strings.

Evaluate the following expressions:

```
> (NUMBERS '(1 2 3))
T

> (NUMBERS '((1) (2) (3)))
NIL

> (NUMBERS '(1 2 ONE TWO))
NIL

> (NUMBERS '(97 98 99))
T
```

The built-in system procedures for list manipulation can be rewritten as recursive LISP procedures. Study the following examples.

Examples

    1. Compute the length of a list (counting top-level expressions only).

```
> (length '(A B C D))
4

> (defun X-LENGTH (L)
1> (cond ((null L) 0)
2>          (T (1+ (X-LENGTH (cdr L))))))
X-LENGTH

> (X-LENGTH '(A B C D))
4
```

    2. Append two lists together.

```
> (append '(A B) '(C D E))
(A B C D E)

> (defun X-APPEND (L M)
1>      (cond ((null L) M)
2>              (T (cons (car L) (X-APPEND (cdr L) M)))))
X-APPEND

> (X-APPEND '(A B) '(C D E))
(A B C D E)
```

3. Find the last top-level element on a list.

```
> (last '(A B C D E))
(E)


> (defun X-LAST (L)
1>       (cond ((null L) NIL)
2>              ((null (cdr L)) L)
2>              (T (X-LAST (cdr L)))))
X-LAST


> (X-LAST '(A B C D E))
(E)
```

4. Find the key expression in an association list.

```
> (assoc 'son '((husband Dan)(son Sam)(daughter Margot)))
(son Sam)

>(defun X-ASSOC (thing L)
1>    (cond ((null L) NIL)
2>           ((equal thing (caar L)) (car L))
2>           (T (X-ASSOC thing (cdr L)))))
X-ASSOC


> (X-ASSOC 'son '((husband Dan)(son Sam)(daughter Margot)))
(son Sam)
```

5. Determine if a symbol is a top-level member of a list.

```
> (member 'B '(A B C D E))
(B C D E)

>(defun X-MEMBER (thing L)
1>    (cond ((null L) NIL)
2>           ((equal thing (car L)) L)
2>           (T (X-MEMBER thing (cdr L)))))
X-MEMBER


> (X-MEMBER 'B '(A B C D E))
(B C D E)
```

6. Reverse the top-level expressions on a list.

```
> (reverse '((A B)(C D)(E F)))
((E F) (C D) (A B))
```

```
>(defun X-REVERSE (L)
1>     (cond ((null L) NIL)
2>            (T (append (X-REVERSE (cdr L)) (list (car L))))))
X-REVERSE

>  (X-REVERSE '((A B) (C D) (E F)))
((E F) (C D) (A B))
```

If we print the intermediate results, we can see the steps taken to derive the solution:

```
>(defun XP-REVERSE (L)
1>     (cond ((null L) NIL)
2>            (T (print (append (XP-REVERSE (cdr L))
5>                              (list (car L))))))))
XP-REVERSE

>  (XP-REVERSE '(1 2 3 4 5))
(5)
(5 4)
(5 4 3)
(5 4 3 2)
(5 4 3 2 1)

>  (XP-REVERSE '((A B) (C D) (E F)))
((E F))
((E F) (C D))
((E F) (C D) (A B))
((E F) (C D) (A B))
```

The procedures presented thus far have worked on the top level of a list. These procedures are referred to as *singly recursive procedures*. For example, the procedure X-REVERSE reverses only the top-level expressions on the list; the nested lists are not manipulated.

Doubly recursive procedures traverse through nested sublists. In order to reverse the expressions on the nested sublists, we need to write a doubly recursive procedure that will reverse the elements on each sublist. We will call the new procedure MIRROR, since it essentially creates a mirror image of a list.

```
>(defun MIRROR (L)
1>     (cond ((null L) NIL)
2>            ((atom L) L)
2>            (T (append (MIRROR (cdr L))
5>                        (list (MIRROR (car L)))))))
MIRROR

>  (MIRROR '((1 2) (3 4)))
((4 3) (2 1))
```

Rather than describe in words how double recursion works, we can modify the procedure MIRROR by inserting print statements. The following definition MIRRORP shows the intermediate steps taken to arrive at the solution.

```
>(defun MIRRORP (L)
1>      (prin1 'DESCEND-WITH) (print L)
1>      (cond ((null L) NIL)
2>            ((atom L) (prin1 'ASCEND-WITH) (print L) L)
2>            (T (print (append (MIRRORP (cdr L))
5>                              (list (MIRRORP (car L)))))))))
MIRRORP

> (MIRRORP '((1 2)(3 4)))
DESCEND-WITH ((1 2)(3 4))
DESCEND-WITH ((3 4))
DESCEND-WITH NIL
DESCEND-WITH (3 4)
DESCEND-WITH (4)
DESCEND-WITH NIL
DESCEND-WITH 4
ASCEND-WITH 4
(4)
DESCEND-WITH 3
ASCEND-WITH 3
(4 3)
((4 3))
DESCEND-WITH (1 2)
DESCEND-WITH (2)
DESCEND-WITH NIL
DESCEND-WITH 2
ASCEND-WITH 2
(2)
DESCEND-WITH 1
ASCEND-WITH 1
(2 1)
((4 3)(2 1))
((4 3)(2 1))
```

EXERCISES

1. Write X-NTH that returns the nth element on a list. For example, (X-NTH 0 '(red blue green violet yellow)) returns red. (X-NTH 2 '(red blue green violet yellow)) rerturns green.

2. Write PALINDROME that creates a list that reads the same backwards or forwards. For example,

   (PALINDROME '(HERE I AM)) returns (HERE I AM I HERE).
   (PALINDROME '(SNOW WHITE LIKES)) returns
   (SNOW WHITE LIKES WHITE SNOW)
   (PALINDROME ' (M A D)) returns (M A D A M)

3. Write a procedure SENTENCE that takes as its argument a list of string elements and returns a concatenated sentence. For example,

   SENTENCE '("Return" "this" "list" "of" "words!")) returns
   ("Return this list of words!")

4. Write KEYS that takes as its argument an association list and returns a list of the keys. For example,

   (KEYS '((husband Dan)(son Sam)(daughter Margot)(kitty Tuxedo))) returns
   (husband son daughter kitty).

ANSWERS

1. (defun X-NTH (num L)
                (cond ((null L) NIL)
                      ((= num 0) (car L))
                      (T (X-NTH (1> num) (cdr L)))))

2. (defun PALINDROME (L)
                (cond ((null L) NIL)
                      ((null (cdr L)) L)
                      (T (append (list (car L))
                                 (PALINDROME (cdr L))
                                 (list (car L))))))

3. (defun SENTENCE (L)
                (cond ((null L) NIL)
                      (T (strcat (car L) (SENTENCE (cdr L))))))

4. (defun KEYS (L)
                (cond ((null L) NIL)
                      (T (append (list (caar L)) (KEYS (cdr L))))))

Appendix A

Summary of XLISP Features*

INTRODUCTION TO XLISP:
AN EXPERIMENTAL OBJECT-ORIENTED LANGUAGE

XLISP is an experimental programming language combining some of the features of LISP with an object-oriented extension capability. It was implemented to allow experimentation with object-oriented programming on small computers. There are currently implementations running on the VAX under VAX/VMS, on the 8088/8086 under MS-DOS, on the 68000 under CP/M-68K, on the Macintosh, on the Atari 520ST, and on the Amiga. It is completely written in the programming language "C" and is easily extended with user-written built-in functions and classes. It is available in source form free of charge to noncommercial users.

Many traditional LISP functions are built into XLISP. In addition, XLISP defines the objects "Object" and "Class" as primitives. "Object" is the only class that has no superclass and hence is the root of the class hierarchy tree. "Class" is the class of which all classes are instances (it is the only object that is an instance of itself).

This document is a brief description of XLISP. It assumes some knowledge of LISP and some understanding of the concepts of object-oriented programming.

A recommended text for learning LISP programming is the already mentioned *LISP* by Winston and Horn. The first edition of this book is based on MACLISP, and the second edition is based on Common LISP. Future versions of XLISP will continue to migrate towards compatibility with Common LISP.

A Note from the Author of XLISP

If you have any problems with XLISP, feel free to contact me for help and advice.* Please remember that since XLISP is available in source form in a high-level language, many users have been making versions available on a variety of machines. The version number you are running is very important, and you must provide it in order to receive a response to your inquiry.

If you find a bug in XLISP, first try to fix the bug yourself using the source code provided. If you are successful in fixing the bug, send the bug report along with the fix to me. If you don't have access to a C compiler or are unable to fix a bug, please send the bug report to me and I'll try to fix it.

Any suggestions for improvements are welcomed. Feel free to extend the language in whatever way suits your needs. However, *please do not release enhanced versions without checking with me first*!! I would like to be the clearing house for new features added to XLISP. If you want to add features for your own personal use, go ahead. But if you want to distribute your enhanced version, contact me first. Please remember that the goal of XLISP is to provide a language to learn and experiment with LISP and object-oriented programming on small computers. I don't want it to get so big that it requires megabytes of memory to run.

XLISP COMMAND LOOP

When XLISP is started, it first tries to load ''init.lsp'' from the default directory. It then loads any files named as parameters on the command line (after appending ''.lsp'' to their names). It then issues the following prompt:

```
>
```

This indicates that XLISP is waiting for an expression to be typed. When an incomplete expression has been typed (one where the left and right parentheses don't match), XLISP changes its prompt to:

```
n>
```

where *n* is an integer indicating how many levels of left parentheses remain unclosed.

---

*David Betz can be contacted at the address given in the documentation file (XLISP.DOC) on your specific XLISP diskette. Please include a stamped, self-addressed envelope with any inquiry.

When a complete expression has been entered, XLISP attempts to evaluate that expression. If the expression evaluates successfully, XLISP prints the result of the evaluation and then returns to the initial prompt waiting for another expression to be typed.

BREAK COMMAND LOOP

When XLISP encounters an error while evaluating an expression, it attempts to handle the error. If the symbol *breakenable* is true, the message corresponding to the error is printed. If the error is correctable, the correction message is printed. If the symbol *tracenable* is true, a trace back is printed. The number of entries printed depends on the value of the symbol *tracelimit*. If this symbol is set to something other than a number, the entire trace back stack is printed. XLISP then enters a read/eval/print loop to allow the user to examine the state of the interpreter in the context of the error. This loop differs from the normal top-level read/eval/print loop in that if the user invokes the function CONTINUE, XLISP will continue from a correctable error. If the user invokes the function CLEAN-UP, XLISP will abort the break loop and return to the top level or the next lower numbered break loop. When in a break loop, XLISP prefixes the break level to the normal prompt.

If the symbol *breakenable* is NIL, XLISP looks for a surrounding errset function. If one is found, XLISP examines the value of the print flag. If this flag is true, the error message is printed. In any case, XLISP causes the errset function call to return NIL. If there is no surrounding errset function, XLISP prints the error message and returns to the top level.

DATA TYPES

There are several different data types available to XLISP programmers.

- ○ lists
- ○ symbols
- ○ strings
- ○ integers
- ○ floats
- ○ objects
- ○ arrays
- ○ file pointers
- ○ SUBRS (built-in functions)
- ○ FSUBRS (special forms)

Another data type is the stream. A *stream* is a list node whose CAR points to the head of a list of integers and whose CDR points to the last list node of the list. An empty stream is a list node whose CAR and CDR are NIL. Each of the integers in the list represents a character in the stream. When a character is read from a stream, the first integer from the head of the list is removed and returned. When a character is written to a stream, the integer representing the character code of the character is appended to the end of the list. When a function indicates that it takes an input source as a parameter, the parameter can either be an input file pointer or a stream. Similarly, when a function indicates that it takes an output sink as a parameter, the parameter can either be an output file pointer or a stream.

THE EVALUATOR

The process of evaluation in XLISP is as follows:

  I. Integers, floats, strings, file pointers, SUBRS, FSUBRS, objects, and arrays evaluate to themselves.
 II. Symbols evaluate to the value associated with their current binding.
III. Lists are evaluated by evaluating the first element of the list and then taking one of the following actions:
   A. If it is a SUBR, the remaining list elements are evaluated and the SUBR is called with these evaluated expressions as arguments.
   B. If it is an FSUBR, the FSUBR is called using the remaining list elements as arguments (unevaluated).
   C. If it is a list:
      1.   If the list is a function closure (a list whose CAR is a lambda expression and whose CDR is an environment list), the CAR of the list is used as the function to be applied and the CDR is used as the environment to be extended with the parameter bindings.
      2.   If the list is a lambda expression, the current environment is used for the function application.
            In either of the two cases above, the remaining list elements are evaluated and the resulting expressions are bound to the formal arguments of the lambda expression. The body of the function is executed within this new binding environment.
      3.   If it is a list and the CAR of the list is MACRO, the remaining list elements are bound to the formal arguments of the macro expression. The body of the function is executed within this new binding environment. The result of this evaluation is considered the *macro expansion*. This result is then evaluated in place of the original expression.
      4.   If it is an object, the second list element is evaluated and used as a message selector. The message formed by combining the selector with the values of the remaining list elements is sent to the object.

LEXICAL CONVENTIONS

The following conventions must be followed when entering XLISP programs:

Comments in XLISP code begin with a semicolon character and continue to the end of the line.

Symbol names in XLISP can consist of any sequence of nonblank, printable characters except the following:

$$( ) \quad ' \quad ` \quad , \quad `` \quad ;$$

Upper- and lower-case characters are not distinguished within symbol names. All lower-case characters are mapped to upper-case on input.

Integer literals consist of a sequence of digits optionally beginning with a " + " or " − ". The range of values an integer can represent is limited by the size of a C "long" on the machine on which XLISP is running.

Floating point literals consist of a sequence of digits optionally beginning with a " + " or " − " and including an embedded decimal point. The range of values a floating point number can represent is limited by the size of a C "float" ("double" on machines with 32-bit addresses) on the machine on which XLISP is running.

Literal strings are sequences of characters surrounded by double quotes. Within quoted strings the " character is used to allow nonprintable characters to be included. The codes recognized are the following:

\\	means the character "\"
\n	means newline
\t	means tab
\r	means return
\f	means form feed
\nnn	means the character whose octal code is nnn

XLISP defines several useful read macros, as follows:

'<expr>	= = (quote <expr>)
#'<expr>	= = (function <expr>)
#(<expr> . . .)	= = an array of the specified expressions
#x<hdigits>	= = a hexadecimal number
#\<char>	= = the ASCII code of the character
`<expr>	= = (backquote <expr>)
,<expr>	= = (comma <expr>)
,@<expr>	= = (comma-at <expr>)

READTABLES

The behavior of the reader is controlled by a data structure called a *readtable*. The reader uses the symbol *READTABLE* to locate the current readtable. This table controls the interpretation of input characters. It is an array with 128 entries, one for each of the ASCII character codes. Each entry contains one of the following things:

NIL	Indicating an invalid character
:CONSTITUENT	Indicating a symbol constituent
:WHITE-SPACE	Indicating a whitespace character
(:TMACRO . fun)	Terminating readmacro
(:NMACRO . fun)	Nonterminating readmacro

In the case of the last two forms, the ''fun'' component is a function definition. This can either be a pointer to a built-in readmacro function or a lambda expression. The function should take two parameters. The first is the input stream, and the second is the character that caused the invocation of the readmacro. The character is passed as an integer. The readmacro function should return NIL to indicate that the character should be treated as white space or a value consed with NIL to indicate that the readmacro should be treated as an occurrence of the specified value. Of course, the readmacro code is free to read additional characters from the input stream.

OBJECTS

Let's define a few terms concerning objects.

○ selector	A symbol used to select an appropriate method
○ message	A selector and a list of actual arguments
○ method	The code that implements a message

Since XLISP was created to provide a simple basis for experimenting with object-oriented programming, one of the primitive data types included is the object. In XLISP, an *object* consists of a data structure containing a pointer to the object's class as well as an array containing the values of the object's instance variables.

Officially, there is no way to see inside an object (look at the values of its instance variables). The only way to communicate with an object is by sending it a message. When the XLISP evaluator evaluates a list, the value of whose first element is an object, it interprets the value of the second element of the list (which must be a symbol) as the message selector. The evaluator determines the class of the receiving object and attempts to find a method corresponding to the message selector in the set of messages defined for that class.

If the message is not found in the object's class and the class has a superclass, the search continues by looking at the messages defined for the superclass. This process continues from one superclass to the next until a method for the message is found. If no method is found, an error occurs.

When a method is found, the evaluator binds the receiving object to the symbol *self*, binds the class in which the method was found to the symbol *msgclass*, and evaluates the method using the remaining elements of the original list as arguments to the method. These arguments are always evaluated prior to being bound to their corresponding formal arguments. The result of evaluating the method becomes the result of the expression.

The "Object" Class

```
Classes:

Object THE TOP OF THE CLASS HIERARCHY

      Messages:

        :show SHOW AN OBJECT'S INSTANCE VARIABLES
                     returns      the object

        :class RETURN THE CLASS OF AN OBJECT
                     returns      the class of the object

        :isnew THE DEFAULT OBJECT INITIALIZATION ROUTINE
                     returns      the object

        :sendsuper <sel> [<args>]. . . SEND SUPERCLASS A MESSAGE
                     <sel>        the message selector
                     <args>       the message arguments
                     returns      the result of sending the message
```

The "Class" CLASS

```
Class THE CLASS OF ALL OBJECT CLASSES  (including itself)

      Messages:

        :new CREATE A NEW INSTANCE OF A CLASS
                     returns      the new class object

        :isnew <ivars> [<cvars>[<super>]] INITIALIZE A NEW CLASS
               <ivars>       the list of instance variable symbols
               <cvars>       the list of class variable symbols
               <super>       the superclass (default is object)
```

```
            returns        the new class object

  :answer <msg> <fargs> <code> ADD A MESSAGE TO A CLASS
                   <msg>          the message symbol
                   <fargs>        the formal argument list
                                  this list is of the form:
                                     ([<farg>]. . .
                                     [&optional [<oarg>]. . .]
                                     [&rest <rarg>]
                                     [&aux [<aux>]. . .]
                                  where
                                  <farg>  a formal argument
                                  <oarg>  an optional argument
                                  <rarg>  bound to rest of the arguments
                                  <aux>  an auxiliary variable
                   <code>         a list of executable expressions
                   returns        the object
```

When a new instance of a class is created by sending the message ":new" to an existing class, the message ":isnew" followed by whatever parameters were passed to the ":new" message is sent to the newly created object.

When a new class is created by sending the ":new" message to the object "class," an optional parameter may be specified indicating the superclass of the new class. If this parameter is omitted, the new class will be subclass of "object." A class inherits all instance variables, class variables, and methods from its superclass.

SYMBOLS

○ self	The current object (within a message context)
○ msgclass	The class in which the current method was found
○ *obarray*	The object hash table
○ *standard-input*	The standard input file
○ *standard-output*	The standard output file
○ *breakenable*	Flag controlling entering break loop on errors
○ *tracenable*	Enable baktrace on errors
○ *tracelimit*	Number of levels of trace back information
○ *evalhook*	User substitute for the evaluator function
○ *applyhook*	(Not yet implemented)
○ *readtable*	The current readtable
○ *unbound*	Indicator for unbound symbols
○ *gc-flag*	Controls the printing of gc messages

EVALUATION FUNCTIONS

(eval <expr>)   EVALUATE AN XLISP EXPRESSION
    <expr>   the expression to be evaluated
    returns   the result of evaluating the expression

(apply <fun> <args>)   APPLY A FUNCTION TO A LIST OF ARGUMENTS
    <fun>   the function to apply (or function symbol)
    <args>   the argument list
    returns   the result of applying the function to the arguments

(funcall <fun> [<arg>] . . .)   CALL A FUNCTION WITH ARGUMENTS
    <fun>   the function to call (or function symbol)
    <arg>   arguments to pass to the function
    returns   the result of calling the function with the arguments

(quote <expr>)   RETURN AN EXPRESSION UNEVALUATED
    <expr>   the expression to be quoted (quoted)
    returns   <expr> unevaluated

(function <expr>)   QUOTE A FUNCTION
    <expr>   the function to be quoted (quoted)
    returns   a function closure

(backquote <expr>)   FILL IN A TEMPLATE
    <expr>   the template
    returns   a copy of the template with comma and comma-at expressions expanded

(lambda <args> [<expr>] . . .)   MAKE A FUNCTION CLOSURE
    <args>   the argument list (quoted)
    <expr>   expressions of the function body
    returns   the function closure

SYMBOL FUNCTIONS

(set <sym> <expr>)   SET THE VALUE OF A SYMBOL
    <sym>   the symbol being set
    <expr>   the new value
    returns   the new value

(setq [<sym> <expr>] . . .)   SET THE VALUE OF A SYMBOL
    <sym>   the symbol being set (quoted)
    <expr>   the new value
    returns   the new value

(setf [<place> <expr>] . . .)   SET THE VALUE OF A FIELD
    <place>   the field specifier (quoted):
        <sym>   set value of a symbol

(car <expr>)	set CAR of a list node
(cdr <expr>)	set CDR of a list node
(nth <n> <expr>)	set NTH CAR of a list
(aref <expr> <n>)	set NTH element of an array
(get <sym> <prop>)	set value of a property
(symbol-value <sym>)	set value of a symbol
(symbol-plist <sym>)	set property list of a symbol

    <expr>   the new value
    returns   the new value

(defun <sym> <fargs> [<expr>] . . .) DEFINE A FUNCTION

(defmacro <sym> <fargs> [<expr>] . . .) DEFINE A MACRO
    <sym>   symbol being defined (quoted)
    <fargs>   list of formal arguments (quoted)
        this list is of the form:

            ([<farg>] . . .
            . .]
            [&rest <rarg>]
            [&aux [<aux>] . . .])
            where

<farg>	is a formal argument
<oarg>	is an optional argument
<rarg>	bound to the rest of the arguments
<aux>	is an auxiliary variable

    <expr>   expressions constituting the body of the function (quoted)
    returns   the function symbol

(gensym [<tag>]) GENERATE A SYMBOL
    <tag>   string or number
    returns   the new symbol

(intern <pname>) MAKE AN INTERNED SYMBOL
    <pname>   the symbol's print name string
    returns   the new symbol

(make-symbol <pname>) MAKE AN UNINTERNED SYMBOL
    <pname>   the symbol's print name string
    returns   the new symbol

(symbol-name <sym>) GET THE PRINT NAME OF A SYMBOL
    <sym>   the symbol
    returns   the symbol's print name

(symbol-value <sym>) GET THE VALUE OF A SYMBOL
    <sym>   the symbol
    returns   the symbol's value

(symbol-plist <sym>) GET THE PROPERTY LIST OF A SYMBOL
    <sym>   the symbol
    returns   the symbol's property list

(hash <sym> <n>)   COMPUTE THE HASH INDEX FOR A SYMBOL
    <sym>   the symbol or string
    <n>   the table size (integer)
    returns   the hash index (integer)

PROPERTY LIST FUNCTIONS

(get <sym> <prop>)   GET THE VALUE OF A PROPERTY
    <sym>   the symbol
    <prop>   the property symbol
    returns   the property value or NIL
(putprop <sym> <val> <prop>)   PUT A PROPERTY ONTO A PROPERTY
                                       LIST
    <sym>   the symbol
    <val>   the property value
    <prop>   the property symbol
    returns   the property value
(remprop <sym> <prop>)   REMOVE A PROPERTY
    <sym>   the symbol
    <prop>   the property symbol
    returns   NIL

ARRAY FUNCTIONS

(aref <array> <n>)   GET THE NTH ELEMENT OF AN ARRAY
    <array>   the array
    <n>   the array index (integer)
    returns   the value of the array element
(make-array <size>)   MAKE A NEW ARRAY
    <size>   the size of the new array (integer)
    returns   the new array

LIST FUNCTIONS

(car <expr>)   RETURN THE CAR OF A LIST NODE
    <expr>   the list node
    returns   the CAR of the list node
(cdr <expr>)   RETURN THE CDR OF A LIST NODE
    <expr>   the list node
    returns   the CDR of the list node

(cxxr <expr>)   ALL CxxR COMBINATIONS

(cxxxr <expr>)   ALL CxxxR COMBINATIONS

(cxxxxr <expr>)   ALL CxxxxR COMBINATIONS

(cons <expr1> <expr2>)   CONSTRUCT A NEW LIST NODE
      <expr1>   the CAR of the new list node
      <expr2>   the CDR of the new list node
      returns   the new list node

(list [<expr>] . . .)   CREATE A LIST OF VALUES
      <expr>   expressions to be combined into a list
      returns   the new list

(append [<expr>] . . .)   APPEND LISTS
      <expr>   lists whose elements are to be appended
      returns   the new list

(reverse <expr>)   REVERSE A LIST
      <expr>   the list to reverse
      returns   a new list in the reverse order

(last <list>)   RETURN THE LAST LIST NODE OF A LIST
      <list>   the list
      returns   the last list node in the list

(member <expr> <list> [<key> <test>])   FIND AN EXPRESSION IN A
                                      LIST
      <expr>   the expression to find
      <list>   the list to search
      <key>   the keyword :test or :test-not
      <test>   the test function (defaults to EQL)
      returns   the remainder of the list starting with the expression

(assoc <expr> <alist> [<key> <test>])   FIND AN EXPRESSION IN AN
                                        A-LIST
      <expr>   the expression to find
      <alist>   the association list
      <key>   the keyword :test or :test-not
      <test>   the test function (defaults to EQL)
      returns   the a-list entry or NIL

(remove <expr> <list> [<key> <test>])   REMOVE AN EXPRESSION
      <expr>   the expression to delete
      <list>   the list
      <key>   the keyword :test or :test-not
      <test>   the test function (defaults to EQL)
      returns   the list with the matching expressions deleted

(length <expr>)   FIND THE LENGTH OF A LIST OR STRING
      returns   the length of the list or string

(nth <n> <list>)   RETURN THE *N*TH ELEMENT OF A LIST
    <n>   the number of the element to return (zero origin)
    <list>   the list
    returns   the NTH element or NIL if the list isn't that long

(nthcdr <n> <list>)   RETURN THE *N*TH CDR OF A LIST
    <n>   the number of the element to return (zero origin)
    <list>   the list
    returns   the NTH CDR or NIL if the list isn't that long

(mapc <fcn> <list1> [<list>] . . .)   APPLY FUNCTION TO SUCCESSIVE
                                          CARS
    <fcn>   the function or function name
    <listn>   a list for each argument of the function
    returns   the first list of arguments

(mapcar <fcn> <list1> [<list>] . . .)   APPLY FUNCTION TO SUCCESSIVE
                                          CARS
    <fcn>   the function or function name
    <listn>   a list for each argument of the function
    returns   a list of the values returned

(mapl <fcn> <list1> [<list>] . . .)   APPLY FUNCTION TO SUCCESSIVE
                                          CDRS
    <fcn>   the function or function name
    <listn>   a list for each argument of the function
    returns   the first list of arguments

(maplist <fcn> <list1> [<list>] . . .)   APPLY FUNCTION TO SUCCESSIVE
                                          CDRS
    <fcn>   the function or function name
    <listn>   a list for each argument of the function
    returns   a list of the values returned

(subst <to> <from> <expr> [<key> <test>])   SUBSTITUTE EXPRES-
                                          SIONS
    <to>   the new expression
    <from>   the old expression
    <expr>   the expression in which to do the substitutions
    <key>   the keyword :test or :test-not
    <test>   the test function (defaults to EQL)
    returns   the expression with substitutions

(sublis <alist> <expr> [<key> <test>])   SUBSTITUTE WITH AN A-LIST
    <alist>   the association list
    <expr>   the expression in which to do the substitutions
    <key>   the keyword :test or :test-not
    <test>   the test function (defaults to EQL)
    returns   the expression with substitutions

DESTRUCTIVE LIST FUNCTIONS

(rplaca <list> <expr>)   REPLACE THE CAR OF A LIST NODE
<list>   the list node
<expr>   the new value for the car of the list node
returns   the list node after updating the car

(rplacd <list> <expr>)   REPLACE THE CDR OF A LIST NODE
<list>   the list node
<expr>   the new value for the CDR of the list node
returns   the list node after updating the CDR

(nconc [<list>] . . .)   DESTRUCTIVELY CONCATENATE LISTS
<list>   lists to concatenate
returns   the result of concatenating the lists

(delete <expr> <list> [<key> <test>])   DELETE AN EXPRESSION FROM
                                        A LIST
<expr>   the expression to delete
<list>   the list
<key>   the keyword :test or :test-not
<test>   the test function (defaults to EQL)
returns   the list with the matching expressions deleted

PREDICATE FUNCTIONS

(atom <expr>)   IS THIS AN ATOM?
<expr>   the expression to check
returns   T if the value is an atom, NIL otherwise

(symbolp <expr>)   IS THIS A SYMBOL?
<expr>   the expression to check
returns   T if the expression is a symbol, NIL otherwise

(numberp <expr>)   IS THIS A NUMBER?
<expr>   the expression to check
returns   T if the expression is a number, NIL otherwise

(null <expr>)   IS THIS AN EMPTY LIST?
<expr>   the list to check
returns   T if the list is empty, NIL otherwise

(not <expr>)   IS THIS FALSE?
<expr>   the expression to check
returns   T if the expression is NIL, NIL otherwise

(listp <expr>)   IS THIS A LIST?
<expr>   the expression to check
returns   T if the value is a list node or NIL, NIL otherwise

(consp <expr>)   IS THIS A NONEMPTY LIST?
    <expr>   the expression to check
    returns   T if the value is a list node, NIL otherwise

(boundp <sym>)   IS THIS SYMBOL BOUND?
    <sym>   the symbol
    returns   T if a value is bound to the symbol, NIL otherwise

(minusp <expr>)   IS THIS NUMBER NEGATIVE?
    <expr>   the number to test
    returns   T if the number is negative, NIL otherwise

(zerop <expr>)   IS THIS NUMBER ZERO?
    <expr>   the number to test
    returns   T if the number is zero, NIL otherwise

(plusp <expr>)   IS THIS NUMBER POSITIVE?
    <expr>   the number to test
    returns   T if the number is positive, NIL otherwise

(evenp <expr>)   IS THIS NUMBER EVEN?
    <expr>   the number to test
    returns   T if the number is even, NIL otherwise

(oddp <expr>)   IS THIS NUMBER ODD?
    <expr>   the number to test
    returns   T if the number is odd, NIL otherwise

(eq <expr1> <expr2>)   ARE THE EXPRESSIONS IDENTICAL?
    <expr1>   the first expression
    <expr2>   the second expression
    returns   T if they are equal, NIL otherwise

(eql <expr1> <expr2>)   ARE THE EXPRESSIONS IDENTICAL? (WORKS
                                        WITH NUMBERS AND STRINGS)
    <expr1>   the first expression
    <expr2>   the second expression
    returns   T if they are equal, NIL otherwise

(equal <expr1> <expr2>)   ARE THE EXPRESSIONS EQUAL?
    <expr1>   the first expression
    <expr2>   the second expression
    returns   T if they are equal, NIL otherwise

CONTROL CONSTRUCTS

(cond [<pair>] . . .)   EVALUATE CONDITIONALLY
    <pair>   pair consisting of:
        (<pred> [<expr>] . . .)
        where
            <pred>   is a predicate expression
            <expr>   is evaluated if the predicate is not NIL

returns	the value of the first expression whose predicate is not NIL

(and [<expr>] . . .)   THE LOGICAL AND OF A LIST OF EXPRESSIONS
    <expr>   the expressions to be ANDed
    returns   NIL if any expression evaluates to NIL, otherwise the value
                of the last expression

(The evaluation of expressions stops after the first expression that evaluates to NIL.)

(or [<expr>] . . .)   THE LOGICAL OR OF A LIST OF EXPRESSIONS
    <expr>   the expressions to be ORed
    returns   NIL if all expressions evaluate to NIL, otherwise the value
                of the first nonNIL expression

(The evaluation of expressions stops after the first expression that does not evaluate to NIL.)

(if <texpr> <expr1> [<expr2>])   EXECUTE EXPRESSIONS CONDITION-
                                   ALLY
    <texpr>   the test expression
    <expr1>   the expression to be evaluated if texpr is nonNIL
    <expr2>   the expression to be evaluated if texpr is NIL
    returns   the value of the selected expression

(case <expr> [<case>] . . .)   SELECT BY CASE
    <expr>   the selection expression
    <case>   pair consisting of:
         (<value> [<expr> . . .)
where

        <value>   is a single expression or a list of ex-
                       pressions (unevaluated)
        <expr>   are expressions to execute if the
                       case matches
        returns   the value of the last expression of
                       the matching case

(let ([<binding>] . . .) [<expr>] . . .)   CREATE LOCAL BINDINGS
(let* ([<binding>] . . .) [<expr>] . . .)   LET WITH SEQUENTIAL BINDING
    <binding>   the variable bindings each of which is either (1) a symbol
                (which is initialized to NIL) or (2) a list whose CAR is a
                symbol and whose CADR is an initialization expression
    <expr>   the expressions to be evaluated
    returns   the value of the last expression

(catch <sym> [<expr>] . . .)   EVALUATE EXPRESSIONS AND CATCH
                             THROW
    <sym>   the catch tag
    <expr>   the expressions to evaluate
    returns   the value of the last throw expression

(throw <sym> [<expr>])   THROW TO A CATCH
    <sym>   the catch tag

<expr>   the value for the catch to return (defaults to NIL)
returns   never returns

LOOPING CONSTRUCTS

(do ([<binding>] . . .) (<texpr> [<rexpr>] . . .) [<expr>] . . .)
(do* ([<binding>] . . .) (<texpr> [<rexpr>] . . .) [<expr>] . . .)
<binding>   the variable bindings each of which is either (1) a symbol
                          (which is initialized to NIL) or (2) a list of the form:
                          (<sym> <init> [<step>])
where:
<sym>   is the symbol to bind
<init>   is the initial value of the symbol
<step>   is a step expression
<texpr>   the termination test expression
<rexpr>   result expresssions (the default is NIL)
<expr>   the body of the loop (treated like an implicit prog)
returns   the value of the last result expression
(dolist (<sym> <expr> [<rexpr>]) [<expr>] . . .)   LOOP THROUGH A
                                                                        LIST
<sym>   the symbol to bind to each list element
<expr>   the list expression
<rexpr>   the result expression (the default is NIL)
<expr>   the body of the loop (treated like an implicit prog)
(dotimes (<sym> <expr> [<rexpr>]) [<expr>] . . .)   LOOP FROM ZERO
                                                                     TO $N-1$
<sym>   the symbol to bind to each value from 0 to $n-1$
<expr>   the number of times to loop
<rexpr>   the result expression (the default is NIL)
<expr>   the body of the loop (treated like an implicit prog)

THE PROGRAM FEATURE

(prog ([<binding>] . . .) [<expr>] . . .)   THE PROGRAM FEATURE
(prog* ([<binding>] . . .) [<expr>] . . .)   PROG WITH SEQUENTIAL
                                                              BINDING
<binding>   the variable bindings each of which is either: (1) a symbol
                          (which is initialized to NIL) or (2) a list whose CAR is a
                          symbol and whose CADR is an initialization expression
<expr>   expressions to evaluate or tags (symbols)
returns   NIL or the argument passed to the return function
(go <sym>)   GO TO A TAG WITHIN A PROG CONSTRUCT
<sym>   the tag (quoted)

returns	never returns

(return [<expr>])   CAUSE A PROG CONSTRUCT TO RETURN A VALUE
        <expr>   the value (defaults to NIL)
        returns   never returns

(prog1 <expr1> [<expr>] . . .)   EXECUTE EXPRESSIONS SEQUENTIALLY
        <expr1>   the first expression to evaluate
        <expr>   the remaining expressions to evaluate
        returns   the value of the first expression

(prog2 <expr1> <expr2> [<expr>] . . .)   EXECUTE EXPRESSIONS SE-
                                        QUENTIALLY
        <expr1>   the first expression to evaluate
        <expr2>   the second expression to evaluate
        <expr>   the remaining expressions to evaluate
        returns   the value of the second expression

(progn [<expr>] . . .)   EXECUTE EXPRESSIONS SEQUENTIALLY
        <expr>   the expressions to evaluate
        returns   the value of the last expression (or NIL)

DEBUGGING AND ERROR HANDLING

(error <emsg> [<arg>])   SIGNAL A NONCORRECTABLE ERROR
        <emsg>   the error message string
        <arg>   the argument expression (printed after the message)
        returns   never returns

(cerror <cmsg> <emsg> [<arg>])   SIGNAL A CORRECTABLE ERROR
        <cmsg>   the continue message string
        <emsg>   the error message string
        <arg>   the argument expression (printed after the message)
        returns   NIL when continued from the break loop

(break [<bmsg> [<arg>])   ENTER A BREAK LOOP
        <bmsg>   the break message string (defaults to **BREAK**)
        <arg>   the argument expression (printed after the message)
        returns   NIL when continued from the break loop

(clean-up)   CLEAN-UP AFTER AN ERROR
        returns   never returns

(continue)   CONTINUE FROM A CORRECTABLE ERROR
        returns   never returns

(errset <expr> [<pflag>])   TRAP ERRORS
        <expr>   the expression to execute
        <pflag>   flag to control printing of the error meessage
        returns   the value of the last expression CONSed with NIL or NIL
                        on error

(baktrace [<n>])   PRINT *N* LEVELS OF TRACE BACK INFORMATION
    <n>   the number of levels (defaults to all levels)
    returns   NIL

(evalhook <expr> <ehook> <ahook> [<env>])   EVALUATE WITH HOOKS
    <expr>   the expression to evaluate
    <ehook>   the value for *evalhook*
    <ahook>   the value for *applyhook*
    <env>   the environment (default is NIL)
    returns   the result of evaluating the expression

ARITHMETIC FUNCTIONS

(truncate <expr>)   TRUNCATES A FLOATING POINT NUMBER TO AN IN-
                      TEGER
    <expr>   the number
    returns   the result of truncating the number

(float <expr>   CONVERTS AN INTEGER TO A FLOATING POINT NUM-
                      BER
    <expr>   the number
    returns   the result of floating the integer

(+ <expr> . . .)   ADD A LIST OF NUMBERS
    <expr>   the numbers
    returns   the result of the addition

(− <expr> . . .)   SUBTRACT A LIST OF NUMBERS OR NEGATE A
                      SINGLE NUMBER
    <expr>   the numbers
    returns   the result of the subtraction

(* <expr> . . .)   MULTIPLY A LIST OF NUMBERS
    <expr>   the numbers
    returns   the result of the multiplication

(/ <expr> . . .)   DIVIDE A LIST OF NUMBERS
    <expr>   the numbers
    returns   the result of the division

(1+ <expr>)   ADD ONE TO A NUMBER
    <expr>   the number
    returns   the number plus one

(1− <expr>)   SUBTRACT ONE FROM A NUMBER
    <expr>   the number
    returns   the number minus one

(rem <expr> . . .)   REMAINDER OF A LIST OF NUMBERS
    <expr>   the numbers
    returns   the result of the remainder operation

(min <expr> . . .)   THE SMALLEST OF A LIST OF NUMBERS
    <expr>   the expressions to be checked
    returns   the smallest number in the list

(max <expr> . . .)   THE LARGEST OF A LIST OF NUMBERS
    <expr>   the expressions to be checked
    returns   the largest number in the list

(abs <expr>)   THE ABSOLUTE VALUE OF A NUMBER
    <expr>   the number
    returns   the absolute value of the number

(random <n>)   COMPUTE A RANDOM NUMBER BETWEEN 1 AND $N-1$
    <n>   the upper bound (integer)
    returns   a random number

(sin <expr>)   COMPUTE THE SINE OF A NUMBER
    <expr>   the floating point number
    returns   the sine of the number

(cos <expr>)   COMPUTE THE COSINE OF A NUMBER
    <expr>   the floating point number
    returns   the cosine of the number

(tan <expr>)   COMPUTE THE TANGENT OF A NUMBER
    <expr>   the floating point number
    returns   the tangent of the number

(expt <x-expr> <y-expr>)   COMPUTE X TO THE Y POWER
    <x-expr>   the floating point number
    <y-expr>   the floating point exponent
    returns   x to the y power

(exp <x-expr>)   COMPUTE E TO THE X POWER
    <x-expr>   the floating point number
    returns   e to the x power

(sqrt <expr>)   COMPUTE THE SQUARE ROOT OF A NUMBER
    <expr>   the floating point number
    returns   the square root of the number

BITWISE LOGICAL FUNCTIONS

(log-and <expr> . . .)   THE BITWISE AND OF A LIST OF NUMBERS
    <expr>   the numbers
    returns   the result of the and operation

(log-ior <expr> . . .)   THE BITWISE INCLUSIVE OR OF A LIST OF NUM-
                               BERS
    <expr>   the numbers
    returns   the result of the inclusive or operation

(log-xor <expr> . . .)   THE BITWISE EXCLUSIVE OR OF A LIST OF NUM-
                          BERS

    <expr>   the numbers

    returns   the result of the exclusive or operation

(log-not <expr>)   THE BITWISE NOT OF A NUMBER

    <expr>   the number

    returns   the bitwise inversion of a number

RELATIONAL FUNCTIONS

The relational functions can be used to compare integers, floating point numbers, or strings.

(< <e1> <e2>)   TEST FOR LESS THAN

    <e1>   the left operand of the comparison

    <e2>   the right operand of the comparison

    returns   the result of comparing <e1> with <e2>

(<= <e1> <e2>)   TEST FOR LESS THAN OR EQUAL TO

    <e1>   the left operand of the comparison

    <e2>   the right operand of the comparison

    returns   the result of comparing <e1> with <e2>

(= <e1> <e2>)   TEST FOR EQUAL TO

    <e1>   the left operand of the comparison

    <e2>   the right operand of the comparison

    returns   the result of comparing <e1> with <e2>

(/= <e1> <e2>)   TEST FOR NOT EQUAL TO

    <e1>   the left operand of the comparison

    <e2>   the right operand of the comparison

    returns   the result of comparing <e1> with <e2>

(>= <e1> <e2>)   TEST FOR GREATER THAN OR EQUAL TO

    <e1>   the left operand of the comparison

    <e2>   the right operand of the comparison

    returns   the result of comparing <e1> with <e2>

(> <e1> <e2>)   TEST FOR GREATER THAN

    <e1>   the left operand of the comparison

    <e2>   the right operand of the comparison

    returns   the result of comparing <e1> with <e2>

STRING FUNCTIONS

(char <string> <index>)   EXTRACT A CHARACTER FROM A STRING

    <string>   the string

<index> the string index (zero relative)
returns the ASCII code of the character

(string <expr>) MAKE A STRING FROM AN INTEGER ASCII VALUE
<expr> the integer
returns a one-character string

(strcat [<expr>] . . .) CONCATENATE STRINGS
<expr> the strings to concatenate
returns the result of concatenating the strings

(substr <expr> <sexpr> [<lexpr>]) EXTRACT A SUBSTRING
<expr> the string
<sexpr> the starting position
<lexpr> the length (default is rest of string)
returns substring starting at <sexpr> for <lexpr>

INPUT/OUTPUT FUNCTIONS

(read [<source> [<eof> [<rflag>]]]) READ AN XLISP EXPRESSION
<source> the input source (default is standard input)
<eof> the value to return on end of file (default is NIL)
<rflag> recursive read flag (default is NIL)
returns the expression read

(print <expr> [<sink>]) PRINT A LIST OF VALUES ON A NEW LINE
<expr> the expressions to be printed
<sink> the output sink (default is standard output)
returns the expression

(prin1 <expr> [<sink>]) PRINT A LIST OF VALUES
<expr> the expressions to be printed
<sink> the output sink (default is standard output)
returns the expression

(princ <expr> [<sink>]) PRINT A LIST OF VALUES WITHOUT QUOTING
<expr> the expressions to be printed
<sink> the output sink (default is standard output)
returns the expression

(terpri [<sink>]) TERMINATE THE CURRENT PRINT LINE
<sink> the output sink (default is standard output)
returns NIL

(flatsize <expr>) LENGTH OF PRINTED REPRESENTATION USING PRIN1
<expr> the expression
returns the length

(flatc <expr>) LENGTH OF PRINTED REPRESENTATION USING PRINC
<expr> the expression
returns the length

FILE I/O FUNCTIONS

(openi <fname>)   OPEN AN INPUT FILE
    <fname>   the file name string or symbol
    returns   a file pointer

(openo <fname>)   OPEN AN OUTPUT FILE
    <fname>   the file name string or symbol
    returns   a file pointer

(close <fp>)   CLOSE A FILE
    <fp>   the file pointer
    returns   NIL

(read-char [<source>])   READ A CHARACTER FROM A FILE OR STREAM
    <source>   the input source (default is standard input)
    returns   the character (integer)

(peek-char [<flag>] [<source>]])   PEEK AT THE NEXT CHARACTER
    <flag>   flag for skipping white space (default is NIL)
    <source>   the input source (default is standard input)
    returns   the character (integer)

(write-char <ch> [<sink>])   WRITE A CHARACTER TO A FILE OR
                          STREAM
    <ch>   the character to put (integer)
    <sink>   the output sink (default is standard output)
    returns   the character (integer)

(read-line) [<source>])   READ A LINE FROM A FILE OR STREAM
    <source>   the input source (default is standard input)
    returns   the input string

SYSTEM FUNCTIONS

(load <fname> [<vflag> [<pflag>]])   LOAD AN XLISP SOURCE FILE
    <fname>   the filename string or symbol
    <vflag>   the verbose flag (default is T)
    <pflag>   the print flag (default is NIL)
    returns   the filename

(transcript [<fname>])   CREATE A FILE WITH A TRANSCRIPT OF A
                          SESSION
    <fname>   file name string or symbol (if missing, close current tran-
                      script)
    returns   T if the transcript is opened, NIL if it is closed

(gc)   FORCE GARBAGE COLLECTION
    returns   NIL

(expand <num>) EXPAND MEMORY BY ADDING SEGMENTS
    <num>   the number of segments to add
    returns   the number of segments added

(alloc <num>) CHANGE NUMBER OF NODES TO ALLOCATE IN EACH
                SEGMENT
    <num>   the number of nodes to allocate
    returns   the old number of nodes to allocate

(mem) SHOW MEMORY ALLOCATION STATISTICS
    returns   NIL

(type-of <expr>) RETURNS THE TYPE OF THE EXPRESSION
    <expr>   the expression to return the type of
    returns   NIL if the value is NIL, otherwise one of the symbols:
                :SYMBOL for symbols
                :OBJECT for objects
                :CONS for conses
                :SUBR for built-ins with evaluated arguments
                :FSUBR for built-ins with unevaluated arguments
                :STRING for strings
                :FIXNUM for integers
                :FLONUM for floating point numbers
                :FILE for file pointers
                :ARRAY for arrays

(peek <addrs>) PEEK AT A LOCATION IN MEMORY
    <addrs>   the address to peek at (integer)
    returns   the value at the specified address (integer)

(poke <addrs> <value>) POKE A VALUE INTO MEMORY
    <addrs>   the address to poke (integer)
    <value>   the value to poke into the address (integer)
    returns   the value

(address-of <expr>) GET THE ADDRESS OF AN XLISP NODE
    <expr>   the node
    returns   the address of the node (integer)

(exit) EXIT XLISP
    returns   never returns

Appendix B

*Graphics and Interface Commands for the IBM PC**

This is a list of IBM-PC specific functions in XLISP version 1.5d and subsequent versions. All of the functions take integers as arguments except where noted. All of the functions return nil.

(dos <cmd>)	EXECUTE A DOS COMMAND
<cmd> the command string	
(get-key)	GET A KEY FROM THE KEYBOARD
(set-cursor <row> <col>)	SET THE CURSOR POSITION
(clear)	CLEAR THE SCREEN
(clear-eol)	CLEAR TO THE END OF THE CURRENT LINE
(clear-eos)	CLEAR TO THE END OF THE SCREEN
(insert-line)	INSERT A LINE
(delete-line)	DELETE A LINE
(insert-char)	INSERT A CHARACTER
(delete-char)	DELETE A CHARACTER

(set-inverse <mode>)   SET INVERSE MODE

   <mode> is T for inverse, NIL for normal

(line <x1> <y1> <x2> <y2>)   DRAW A LINE

                                            DRAW A POINT

(point <x> <y>)   DRAW A CIRCLE

(circle <x> <y> <radius>)   SET THE ASPECT RATIO FOR CIRCLES

(aspect-ratio <x> <y>)

(colors <color> <palette> <background>)   SET THE DISPLAY COLORS

                                            SET THE DISPLAY MODE

(mode <mode>)

Appendix C

Graphics
and Interface Commands
for the Macintosh*

MACINTOSH QUICKDRAW GRAPHICS FUNCTIONS

(show-graphics)   SHOW THE GRAPHICS WINDOW
    returns   NIL

(hide-graphics)   HIDE THE GRAPHICS WINDOW
    returns   NIL

(clear-graphics)   CLEAR THE GRAPHICS WINDOW
    returns   NIL

(showpen)   SHOW THE DRAWING PEN
    returns   NIL

(hidepen)   HIDE THE DRAWING PEN
    returns   NIL

(getpen)   GET THE LOCATION OF THE DRAWING PEN
    returns   location of the pen as a dotted pair

(pensize <w> <h>)   SET THE PEN SIZE
    <w>   the width of the pen (integer)
    <h>   the height of the pen (integer)
    returns   NIL

(penmode <mode>)   SET THE DRAWING MODE
      <mode>   drawing mode (integer)
      returns   NIL

(penpat <pat>)   SET THE PEN PATTERN
      <pat>   pattern (list of integers)
      returns   NIL

(pennormal)   SET THE PEN BACK TO NORMAL
      returns   NIL

(move <dh> <dv>)   MOVE THE PEN (RELATIVE)
      <dh>   change in horizontal position (integer)
      <dv>   change in vertical position (integer)
      returns   NIL

(moveto <h> <v>)   MOVE THE PEN (ABSOLUTE)
      <h>   horizontal position (integer)
      <v>   vertical position (integer)
      returns   NIL

(line <dh> <dv>)   DRAW A LINE (RELATIVE)
      <dh>   change in horizontal position (integer)
      <dv>   change in vertical position (integer)
      returns   NIL

(lineto <h> <v>)   DRAW A LINE (ABSOLUTE)
      <h>   horizontal position (integer)
      <v>   vertical position (integer)
      returns   NIL

MACINTOSH TOOLBOX INTERFACE FUNCTIONS

Here are some functions that have been added to XLISP in the version 1.5b release. They are specific to the Macintosh version and are intended to provide a low-level interface to the Macintosh toolbox. They are *very* dangerous! Any incorrect use of these functions could easily result in a system crash or disk file corruption. Use these functions carefully, and make sure you back up your files before trying anything.

(toolbox <trap> [<arg>]. . .)   CALL A TOOLBOX PROCEDURE (NO
                                           RETURN VALUE)

(toolbox-16 <trap> [<arg>]. . .)   CALL A TOOLBOX FUNCTION WITH
                                           A 16-BIT VALUE

(toolbox-32 <trap> [<arg>]. . .)   CALL A TOOLBOX FUNCTION WITH
                                           A 32-BIT VALUE

All of the functions above make it possible to call the stack-based toolbox routines. All of the arguments are integers (FIXNUMS), and they are all interpreted as 16-bit values. If you need to pass a 32-bit address, you'll have to take it apart and pass it as two separate 16-bit arguments. Pass only as many arguments as the toolbox routine expects. Additional arguments won't be ignored. *They will cause a system bomb!*

The first argument of each of these functions is the 16-bit trap word used by assembly language programmers to call the toolbox routine. You can specify it in hex if you use the reader facility for entering hex numbers:

    #xA954 will read as the decimal number 43348
    #x100   will read as the decimal number 256

The remaining arguments are pushed onto the stack before the trap word is executed. They are all treated as 16-bit integers.

The value returned is the value left on the stack by the toolbox routine. Any toolbox routines that return values in reference parameters need to be handled by passing the address of a place to store the result. You can do this by some fancy manipulation of the ADDRESS-OF function. *Be careful.*

(NewHandle \<size>)	ALLOCATE A RELOCATABLE BLOCK OF MEMORY
(NewPtr \<size>)	ALLOCATE A NONRELOCATABLE BLOCK OF MEMORY

These functions allocate memory. The first returns a handle to the space allocated and the second returns a pointer to the space. In both cases, the size is an integer. The result is also an integer whose value is the 32-bit address of the handle or allocated space.

(HiWord \<num>)	RETURN THE HIGH ORDER 16 BITS OF AN INTEGER
(LoWord \<num>)	RETURN THE LOW ORDER 16 BITS OF AN INTEGER

These functions simplify separating a 32-bit value into two 16-bit halves. They are useful where it is necessary to pass 32-bit pointers or handles to the toolbox interface functions.

command-window	ADDRESS OF THE COMMAND WINDOW (FIXNUM)
graphics-window	ADDRESS OF THE GRAPHICS WINDOW (FIXNUM)

These global variables contain the WindowPtrs to the command and graphics windows in the standard XLISP user interface.

    (peek <adr>)   PEEK AT A VALUE IN MEMORY
    (poke <adr> <val>)   POKE A VALUE INTO MEMORY

In both cases above, the address is an integer (FIXNUM). The number of bits that are significant in the address depends on the host processor. For the 68000 (the processor in the Macintosh), FIXNUMs are 32 bits and so are addresses, so all bits are significant. The value returned by PEEK and POKE is also an integer. The number of significant bits is determined by the size of an ''int'' in the underlying ''C'' implementation. For the Macintosh, 16 bits are significant.

    (address-of <expr>)   GET THE MACHINE ADDRESS OF AN XLISP
                              NODE

This function returns the location in memory of the specified XLISP value. It returns an integer (FIXNUM) whose value is the address of the node used internally to represent the value.

    (read-char-no-hang)   READ A CHARACTER FROM THE KEYBOARD
                              WITHOUT WAITING

This function checks if a character is available from the keyboard. If a character is available, READ-CHAR-NO-HANG returns the character without echoing it. The character is returned as an integer whose value is the ASCII code of the character. If no character is available, the function returns NIL.

If you need to call any of the register-based toolbox routines, you will have to resort to something similar to the following example, in which we are building an array containing machine code and then fooling XLISP into thinking that it is a built-in function. This is also *very* dangerous! *Use with caution!*

```
(defun make-subr (code &aux subr hunk adrs)) ; (make-subr <code-list >)
MAKE A SUBR NODE

(setq hunk (NewPtr (* (length code) 2)))       ;allocate some space
                                               ;for the code

(dotimes (i (length (code))                     ;stuff the code into
                                               ;the space

  (poke (+ hunk i i) (car code))
  (setq code (cdr code)))
```

```
(setq subr (+ 1 1))                    ;create a node we can
                                       ;convert to a SUBR

(setq adrs (address-of subr))

(poke adrs #x100)                      ;initialize the node
                                       ;type (SUBR = 1)

(poke (+ adrs 2) (HiWord hunk))        ;store the address of the
                                       ;code space

(poke (+ adrs 4) (LoWord hunk)

                                       ;(subr) return the new SUBR node

(setq beep (make-subr '(              ;try it out with the
                                       ;SysBeep(10 test

#x3F3C #x000A                          ;move.w #10, -(SP)
#xA9C8                                 ;_SysBeep
#x4280                                 ;clr.1 DO ;return nil to XLISP
#x4E75))))                             ;rts
```

ORDERING THE DISKETTE

The XLISP interpreter is available on diskette through the Boston Computer Society Artificial Interest Group, which has a software exchange library. The MS/PCDOS diskette requires a minimum of 128K RAM.

To obtain the diskette, please send a check or money order payable to the Boston Computer Society for $10 ($7 if you are a BCS member) to

> The Boston Computer Society
> One Center Plaza
> Boston, Mass. 02108

> Attention: Artificial Intelligence Interest Group

Please specify that you would like disk #1 XLISP.

Index